DIVINE RIGHT

DIVINE RIGHT

by Peter Whelan

WARNER/CHAPPELL PLAYS

LONDON

A Warner Music Group Company

DIVINE RIGHT
First published in 1996
by Warner/Chappell Plays Ltd
129 Park Street, London W1Y 3FA

Copyright © 1996 by Peter Whelan

The author asserts his moral right to be identified as the author of the work.

ISBN 0 85676 222 9

This play is protected by Copyright. According to Copyright Law, no public performance or reading of a protected play or part of that play may be given without prior authorization from Warner/Chappell Plays Ltd., as agent for the Copyright Owners.

From time to time it is necessary to restrict or even withdraw the rights of certain plays. **It is therefore essential to check with us before making a commitment to produce a play.**

NO PERFORMANCE MAY BE GIVEN WITHOUT A LICENCE

AMATEUR PRODUCTIONS
Royalties are due at least fourteen days prior to the first performance. A royalty quotation will be issued upon receipt of the following details:

Name of Licensee
Play Title
Place of Performance
Dates and Number of Performances
Audience Capacity
Ticket Prices

PROFESSIONAL PRODUCTIONS
All enquiries regarding professional rights should be addressed to The Agency (London) Ltd, 24 Pottery Lane, Holland Park, London W11 4LZ.

OVERSEAS PRODUCTIONS
Applications for productions overseas should be addressed to our local authorized agents. Further details are listed in our catalogue of plays, published every two years, or available from Warner/Chappell Plays at the address above.

CONDITIONS OF SALE
This book is sold subject to the condition that it shall not by way of trade or otherwise be re-sold, hired out, circulated or distributed without prior consent of the Publisher. **Reproduction of the text either in whole or part and by any means is strictly forbidden.**

Printed by Commercial Colour Press, London E7

DIVINE RIGHT was first performed at the Birmingham Repertory Theatre, Birmingham, on 19th April, 1996, with the following cast:

RON MCNEIL	Robin Pirongs
GWEN PAGE	Rina Mahoney
JOHN REESEDALE	Leo Wringer
ELLEN GORSE	Kate Seaward
THE PRINCE	William Mannering
JUNIOR MINISTER	Adam Smethurst
MADAM SPEAKER	Sally Knyvette
JO BENYON	Mary Jo Randle
PRIME MINISTER	Paul Connolly
LEADER OF THE OPPOSITION	David Phelan
CARL POINTER	Ian Gelder
LYDIA WEST	Annie Farr
SARAH POINTER	Sally Knyvette
SIR JAMES HEANEY	Joe Melia
SKIP	Christopher Trezise
LADY CONSTANCE	Rina Mahoney
GIERSON	Gary Powell
KERRIGAN-LARBY	Mark Brignal
WEMBLEY STADIUM DIRECTOR	Leo Wringer
EDIE	Kate Seaward
DES	Gary Powell
RORKIE	Robin Pirongs
JILL	Rina Mahoney
GREG	Adam Smethurst
POLICE OFFICER	Gary Powell
SHOP MANAGER	Leo Wringer
RENA	Annie Farr
MARK HARGREAVES	Mark Brignal
JENNY	Sally Knyvette

Directed by Bill Alexander
Designed by Kit Surrey
Lighting designed by Bob Bryan

CAST
(in order of appearance)

Ron McNeil, Royal detective
Gwen Page, TV head of make-up
John Reesedale, TV Presenter
Ellen Gorse, TV Director
The Prince
A Junior Minister
Madam Speaker
Jo Benyon, Labour MP
Prime Minister (Labour)
Leader of the Opposition (Tory)
Carl Pointer, Tory MP
Lydia West, a schoolteacher
Sarah Pointer, Tory councillor, Carl's wife
Sir James Heaney, a wealthy industrialist in his 70's
Skip, the Prince's brother
Lady Constance, the Prince's girlfriend
Gierson, a gritty Labour backbencher, MP
Kerrigan-Larby, Tory MP
A Director of Wembley Stadium
Motorist in cafe
Edie, an old lady
Des, a fascist heavy
Rorkie, his mate
Jill, Sir James's secretary
A Chauffeur
Greg
A Police Officer
A Shop Manager
Rena, a bag lady
Mark Hargreaves, middle-aged shopper
Jenny, Lydia's neighbour

The play takes place in the year 2000 in London and the Midlands

FOREWORD

It was Bill Alexander, artistic director of Birmingham Rep, who gave me the theme for this play. "I think a playwright today should be writing about the end of the monarchy and the beginning of a British republic . . . ", he said one fine day in summer '94. He'd been to the Times/Charter 88 conference on the monarchy the previous autumn . . . so we have a chain of events at work.

I know we'd have both said at that time that it wasn't a subject at the top of people's minds. Despite the depressing behaviour of the young Royals, public support for the monarchy didn't seem so different from that of the previous two decades. All the same I could sense, the moment he spoke, that there had to be a touch of prophecy there . . .

It's one thing to have a theme and another to see the play in it. When I did I was cautious, setting the endgame crisis in the monarchy five years ahead, at the millennium. I finished the play in summer '95 . . . and still the dam hadn't broken. Then came the true confessions of our queen of hearts, in front of the nation, on TV, and suddenly, as Di holed the Royal yacht below the water line, the unstoppable debate began. From Dimbleby's "Question Time" audiences to the readers of the Sun, dissatisfaction with the monarchy burst out as though hit by a bouncing bomb. The Independent on Sunday became avowedly republican (as the Economist had been for some time). The Guardian and Observer teetered on the edge.

I began to think the republic would be declared before we could get to opening night. But these things ebb as well as flow . . .

I've been a republican in spirit since, at eighteen, I had to take the mandatory oath to the king (this was 1949) when I did military service. It really disturbed me that I was expected to shoot and be shot at for the sake of this remote and empty symbol. I went away right afterwards and took my own secret oath to loved ones, friends, parliament and country . . . not some distant millionaire on a balcony.

But I feel more republican than I feel anti-royal. We've put the royal family in an impossible position. We want the mystery maintained but seize avidly on every tit-bit that exposes their private lives. We have destroyed them as much as they've destroyed themselves . . . and it's high time we faced the consequences.

And let's remember that, if the monarchy is declining in popularity, Westminster politics have declined even further in the nation's esteem. Parliamentarians seem more and more helpless in the face of secretive, arrogant, over-weening government. We have, in the words of Lord Hailsham, an "elective dictatorship". I hope for a republican head of state who, as well as being titular head, will have powers to watch over open government and standards in public life. It follows that I believe in the people electing that head of state . . . not parliament.

It's love of this country and wanting life to get better for us all that makes me republican. I also happen to think it would be more colourful and more fun. Look what the Americans do on the 4th of July . . . or the French on Bastille Day. We have long since lost, under the monarchy, any sense of true national celebration. But for that we need to be citizens, not subjects.

Peter Whelan
April, 1996

ACT ONE

Scene One

The make-up department of a major TV studio where the PRINCE *will shortly arrive to make ready for his discussion programme.*

RON MCNEIL, *Royal Detective, gives the room a final inspection, watched by Head of Make-Up,* GWEN PAGE.

RON *speaks on his mobile.*

RON	027 McNeil . . . We're clear . . . Yes, clean bill of health . . . When you're ready. Right.
	(*He puts the mobile away and smiles at* GWEN.)
GWEN	What's he like?
RON	Now I bet you've been trying *not* to ask me that for the past ten minutes.
GWEN	It's the cliche question, isn't it? I hate cliches. What's he like?
RON	What shall I say? . . . a complete gentleman.
GWEN	Yes, but what's he like?
RON	You're going to find out soon enough when he's in your chair. You'll be closer to him than anyone except his own mother . . .
GWEN	That's what disturbs me. Does he worry about how he looks?
RON	Not seriously. No more than the rest of us. He doesn't seem overly grateful for his nose.
GWEN	Why not?
RON	I don't know . . . I'm not that sold on mine.

GWEN	They say he's not as polite as his parents.
RON	Oh he'll be polite . . . even if he doesn't feel polite. Make no mistake . . . he's sharper, yes . . . but still a prince. He'll chat, even though he may not feel like chatting. He'll be interested . . . even if he's bored. He'll be pleased even if he feels far from pleased. And I don't mean he's putting it on. He's like that normally.
GWEN	You mean you can't tell what he's actually thinking.
RON	I mean he's the same in private. I've been his detective for five years now . . . I see him amongst his family. They all have the royal manner . . . and the royal manner is a kind of schizophrenia . . . split personality. I mean, when the queen gets her toe stuck in the bath tap she's not quite the same woman who opens parliament. Even though, privately, they both have the same effect on her. Now he has the royal manner . . . but . . . in his case it's a form of schizophrenia where the one personality is exactly the same as the other . . .

(GWEN *acknowledges the leg-pull.*)

GWEN	I'll just have to wait till your book comes out won't I?
RON	Oh, I won't write a book.
GWEN	Everyone who works for them says they won't write a book.
RON	That's why I'm saying it. (*Pause.*) It's an honour, you know . . . me doing what I do. I never really get used to the thought that it's me . . . here . . . with the man who will be king one day. And now, of course, it could be sooner than we think . . . (*His mobile bleeps. He takes it. Into phone.*) 027 McNeil . . . Yes? Fine. Will do. (*Pockets the mobile. Speaks to* GWEN.) Action . . .

(*Enter the interviewer/anchorman,* JOHN REESEDALE *and executive producer,* ELLEN GORSE.)

JOHN He's just driven in. You ready Gwen?

GWEN I think I've been ready the whole day!

JOHN Alright sergeant?

RON Absolutely sir.

ELLEN (*to* GWEN) Your department's out there by the lift, waiting to be introduced . . .

(*There is a feeling that* ELLEN *is wanting them to leave so that she can talk to* JOHN.)

GWEN Right . . .

(*She inspects herself quickly in the mirror and exits, followed by* MCNEIL, *who detects a stormy atmosphere.*)

JOHN Look . . . I will not argue the toss just before we're about to get underway. Ellen . . . I have a job to do . . .

ELLEN It's not the format we discussed.

JOHN That was before you went off conferencing in Barcelona. If you think it such a big deal you should have sent someone else and been here for decisions. Could we can it now? I have an interview to think about!

ELLEN But it isn't an interview! What we decided was an interview. You've turned it into a discussion . . .

JOHN As he wanted it . . .

ELLEN A debate!

JOHN Yes!

ELLEN	A confrontational debate!
JOHN	I don't think they come in any other flavour! There are two sides . . . you confront!
ELLEN	But on the one side you have HRH . . . on the other you've got three anti-monarchists!
JOHN	That's how he wanted it.
ELLEN	Well I know we're in the year 2000 . . .
JOHN	Indeed . . .
ELLEN	And I know Birtism is dead . . .
JOHN	Depends on what you mean by dead. Or Birtism. If you mean gutless government arse-licking masquerading as quasi-marketeering role play then it's very much alive . . .
ELLEN	I have to fight your corner, John! I take the stick. I keep the politicians away from you when they're screaming for more balance.
JOHN	You can't have *more* balance . . . you either have it or you don't.
ELLEN	They'll say you don't!
JOHN	All politicians want balance as long as it's tilted in their favour. It's too late Ellen. The decision's made. I mean you're Executive Producer . . . don't give me a hard time. Talk to them upstairs!
ELLEN	I suppose it's me getting emotional about it. Comes of standing on the Mall years ago waving my little Union Jack to watch the golden coach go by! How did they get into such a mess? That farce of a divorce — and it's all gone downhill from there. And here you have a prince, barely eighteen, and already we're putting him in the dock!

JOHN	His choice. He knows what he's doing. Look . . . we've got a member of the Royal Family engaging in public debate about the monarchy. We're making a bit of history. For Christ's sake rise to the level of great events!
ELLEN	Will his father renounce the succession?
	(She says this as though it is commonly assumed that he might.)
JOHN	Oh yes . . .
ELLEN	When? What's your guess?
JOHN	Within days. *(Nods.)* True.
	(MCNEIL *enters and gestures silently that the* PRINCE *is now arriving.* ELLEN *and* JOHN *exit.* MCNEIL *remains, looking out through the open door, professionally watchful, observing the scene as the* PRINCE *is generally introduced outside. We hear the exchanges.)*
VOICE	*(off)* Ellen Gorse and John Reesedale you know, sir.
ELLEN	*(off)* Your highness . . .
PRINCE	*(off)* How are you?
JOHN	*(off)* Your highness . . .
PRINCE	*(off)* John! Hello again . . .
VOICE	*(off)* This is Gwen Page, our head of make-up.
PRINCE	*(off)* Ah! You're to do the deed? Make me look good!
GWEN	*(off)* That's right, your highness . . .
PRINCE	*(off)* Mission impossible?
	(We hear laughter from the department. MCNEIL *smiles at the way the* PRINCE *is handling it.)*

GWEN	(*off*) No sir . . . not at all. May I introduce Jill Nolan . . . Mark Vosper . . . Margaret Snow . . . Ashar Pradesh . . .

(*We hardly hear this low-key conversation.*)

PRINCE	(*off*) What are you on at the moment?
ASHAR	(*off*) "Black Hole", your highness . . . Science Fiction series.
PRINCE	(*off*) I know it. All those latex masks . . . that's what I need!

(*Again laughter, amongst which we lose the final brief remarks as the Controller hands the* PRINCE *over.* GWEN *now enters the make-up room, followed by the* PRINCE *who surveys it amusedly. He wears an immaculate light grey suit.*)

GWEN	My make-up room, sir . . .
PRINCE	So this is where it happens? Lot of reflections . . . a bit unnerving to see so many images of oneself . . .
GWEN	Not if you were an actor, sir. You wouldn't be able to get enough of it.
PRINCE	The back view's rather disturbing. Almost as though you're masquerading as someone else . . .
GWEN	I always say this is the one place where you can really see things clearly.
PRINCE	Good . . .

(*He seems to put a hidden purpose into the word that attracts* MCNEIL'S *attention. The* PRINCE *smiles at him.*)

And excellent for Sergeant McNeil. He likes to keep me well in view . . .

(ELLEN *and* JOHN *have returned.* JOHN *hands the* PRINCE *a script.*)

ELLEN
Would you excuse us sir . . . before you get started.

JOHN
This is the final list of possible questions, sir. Only one different from the one you already have. This last one. "Should the Royal Family be reduced in size?"

PRINCE
Ah yes . . . I have been putting on a bit of weight recently.

(JOHN *and* GWEN *laugh.* ELLEN, *very tense, laughs a beat late.*)

JOHN
I don't know how it didn't get on the original list . . . if you recall, we did touch upon it.

PRINCE
Yes I'm as ready or not ready for that one as I'm likely to be.

JOHN
But additionally there's now the question of your father's possible renunciation of the succession.

ELLEN
We don't have to ask it . . .

(*The* PRINCE *detects the friction between them.*)

PRINCE
Oh you must. I think tomorrow's headlines would be pretty scathing if you didn't. And I'd be pretty abject if I couldn't say something about it. Go ahead.

(JOHN *would really like to discuss it further but the* PRINCE *seems to have closed that subject.*)

ELLEN
Well . . . we'll leave you sir . . . and see you in a little while.

(ELLEN *and* JOHN *exit.* MCNEIL *sits quietly to one side. The* PRINCE *sits in the chair, and* GWEN *puts the sheet around him. He is deep in thought for a moment . . . as* GWEN *is aware.*)

PRINCE So . . . is it an all-over job? Facial retread?

GWEN No . . . not at all. Just the forehead . . . chin . . . take back these shadows under the eyes . . .

PRINCE Ah yes. A few late nights this week. What about the nose?

GWEN Just powder.

(*She makes a start on his forehead.*)

PRINCE Between you and me, I've never felt I looked the part. I don't look like a prince. My brother used to say I looked like a double glazing salesman . . . but then I've never met a double glazing salesman, so I wouldn't know. Olivier looked like a prince in the film of Henry the Fifth. Even Branagh . . . of course, the thing about Olivier was that he could change his nose.

GWEN Head up a little sir . . .

PRINCE How d'you do scars?

GWEN You buy them by the dozen . . . here.

(*She produces a pack.*)

Plastic, you see . . . and when it's stuck on you dissolve the edges with this.

(*Shows a bottle. Continues with make-up.*)

PRINCE Marvellous . . . I've only ever done make-up in school plays. I overdid it hideously but I was always depressed the way people always recognised me instantly. Now how would I change my appearance so that even Sergeant McNeil wouldn't know me in the street? False whiskers?

RON · They'd have to be good ones to get by me sir . . .

(*His mobile bleeps. He takes it out.*)

Excuse me sir. (*In phone.*) 027 McNeil . . . yes.

(*We hear only a murmur as he takes the call outside the door.* GWEN *carries on working.*)

GWEN · Well in public I think the main thing is not make-up but doing the unexpected. I knew a famous actor. I won't say who. His private life got in a tangle and he wanted to be unrecognised . . . so he just wore a dirty old coat and a piece of sticking plaster over one eyebrow . . . as though he'd been in a fight.

PRINCE · And it worked?

GWEN · Oh yes. I'm sure some people might say: doesn't that man look like that actor . . . but they wouldn't really think it was him. You don't expect to see him like that . . .

PRINCE · Well if one day you pass me on the street with a dirty old coat and a sticking plaster over one eye don't let on will you?

(MCNEIL *comes back, putting the mobile away.*)

RON · Sir Edward, sir . . . from the Palace. He asked if you'd call him before the filming.

PRINCE · Before . . .

RON · Yes sir.

PRINCE · Did it sound like bad news?

RON · I don't know sir.

PRINCE · Remind me will you?

RON · Yes sir.

	(GWEN *works away in silence, then pauses and turns away, showing emotion.*)
PRINCE	Are you upset?
GWEN	It's just the pressure they put on you sir. It upsets me, yes.
PRINCE	All jobs have pressure. I'm sure yours does.
GWEN	Yes . . . but I chose mine, sir . . .
	(*She looks tense, as though she feels she's stepped too far out of line. But she has struck a chord with the* PRINCE. *As* GWEN *goes on working on him, fade to black.*)

Scene Two

Westminster. The debating chamber of Parliament. A moderate attendance of members prior to Prime Minister's question time. A JUNIOR HOME OFFICE MINISTER *on the government (Labour) front bench is on his feet, trying to make himself heard against a good-humoured outburst of partisan feeling.*

MINISTER	If I may answer the honourable gentleman . . .
	(*More jeers and cheers.*)
	If I may answer the honourable gentleman . . .
SPEAKER	Order . . . this is the last Home Office question. Please let it be answered . . .
	(*The din subsides.*)
MINISTER	The honourable gentleman asks, Madam Speaker, whether the nation should be grateful to the Conservatives for the idea of the National Lottery because of the funding it has provided for this year's millennium celebrations. Well, I remind him that the nation had already shown its gratitude to the

Tories in the run-up to the millennium by voting in a Labour government . . .

(*More reaction. The* PRIME MINISTER *enters.*)

Which, Madam Speaker, now that the millennim is here, gives them a double cause for celebration!

(*As the* PRIME MINISTER *enters, more and more members have hurried in to find their seats.*)

SPEAKER Question to the Prime Minister . . . Jo Benyon . . .

(JO BENYON, *Labour backbencher, rises.*)

JO Will my right honourable friend please give the house a list of his engagements for today?

PM This morning, Madam Speaker, I had meetings with colleagues and others. In addition to my duties in the House I shall be holding further meetings today.

JO Would the Prime Minister find time to discuss the holding of a full and thorough debate on the monarchy? Since he must be aware that every newspaper, TV and radio station is speculating that the Prince of Wales is about to renounce his right to the throne . . .

(*Uproar.*)

SPEAKER Order . . . order! . . . Order. Honourable members must not waste time in pointless shouting . . . Jo Benyon . . .

JO And is he aware that while we sit here, unable to debate the subject, the next heir to the throne is in a TV studio recording an interview on the future of the monarchy, which is now looking so insecure that the republican alternative must be discussed . . .

(*More uproar . . . but it subsides as the* PRIME MINISTER *gets to his feet.*)

PM Certainly my honourable friend is right . . . there has been a great deal of speculation . . . but I don't know what she means by the 'insecurity' of the monarchy. The queen reigns . . .

(*Loyal cheers.*)

She reigns and long may she reign. She will reign into the new millennium . . .

(*Cheers.*)

Much loved and cherished by her people . . . and the overwhelming majority of this side of the house . . .

TORY MPS Count them! How many? Are you sure?

PM Any questions we have about the monarchy only concern its efficiency and its modernisation for the coming years. Our radical programme of constitutional reform is entirely consistent with a continuing popular role for monarchy with a slimmed-down civil list. As for the Prince of Wales, he deserves our sympathy . . . but his son's interview was scheduled weeks ago and it seems to me entirely appropriate that, having reached his eighteenth birthday he should wish to discuss the future of the monarchy and I, for one, will be most interested in what he has to say.

(*The* PM *sits.* JO BENYON *is on her feet.*)

JO Madam Speaker! I have called for a debate on the republican alternative! He hasn't answered . . .

SPEAKER When honourable members are supposed to ask one question and turn it into six questions they shouldn't be surprised if they're not all

	answered . . . Oh . . . the Prime Minister wishes to answer. Count yourself lucky.
PM	Well Madam Speaker . . . the honourable lady is well known for her republican views and she seems to have become the spokesperson for the small group that shares her views . . .
Jo	Double in size in the last three weeks!
Speaker	Order! D'you want your question answered or not? Prime Minister . . .
PM	I was going to suggest that the most suitable place for a discussion of her views is the Constitutional Committee.

(*He sits. The* LEADER OF THE OPPOSITION *rises.*)

L Opp	On a point of order, Madam Speaker, the Constitutional Committee is in being to examine the composition of the House of Lords. It was never the intention of this House to make it a sounding board for a faddish, trendy irrelevance totally outside its terms of reference. The Prime Minister cannot have it both ways. He cannot profess the Labour Party's loyalty to the queen and at the same time issue an open invitation for some of his party to indulge in republican arguments. I say this to him: if republicanism is discussed on that committee than members of it from this side of the House will, I'm sure, wish to be absent.

(CARL POINTER, *Tory backbencher, rises.*)

Carl	Not all of them, Madam Speaker!
Speaker	Order! Mr Pointer . . . will you please sit down!
Carl	I'd like my right honourable friend to know . . .
Speaker	The honourable gentleman has not been called . . .

ACT ONE

CARL ... some on this side of the house believe in true meritocracy ... which, is incompatible with monarchy ...

(*He has to shout this through howls from his own side and jeers from the other.*)

SPEAKER Will the gentleman sit so that we can get on?

CARL I believe we should discuss republicanism and have a duty to do so!

SPEAKER I warn the honourable gentleman ...

CARL Madam Speaker. If the Prince of Wales abdicates then the future of the monarchy is to be decided by an eighteen year old just out of school!

SPEAKER If the honourable gentleman persists I will have him removed from the chamber.

(CARL *sits.*)

CARL I'm sorry Madam Speaker ... I feel strongly ...

SPEAKER We have a house full of members who feel strongly ... especially when these proceedings are being transmitted live on TV ... and hold up other members who are trying to question the Prime Minister ... Mr Kerrigan-Larby ...

(*Hopeful members sit, leaving a Tory member,* KERRIGAN-LARBY, *on his feet.*)

KERRIGAN-LARBY Will the Prime Minister, when he visits Brussels shortly, take a further step in the creating of a European navy?

(*We fade on Parliament as the* PRIME MINISTER *rises to answer.*)

PM If we are talking of the European Naval Task Force then the answer is 'none'. It will not be on the agenda at the forthcoming meeting of heads of state. However . . .

(*We have gone into black with the sound of members' footsteps echoing in the corridors of Westminster Palace.*)

Scene Three

The lobby near the debating chamber, a short time later. The LEADER OF THE OPPOSITION *and* CARL POINTER *in a hurried conversation.*

L OPP	I wasn't overjoyed by that Carl!
CARL	It had to be said . . .
L OPP	We've talked about it! Where loyalty to the crown is concerned I don't want anyone to be able to get a bus ticket between us . . .
CARL	With all respect . . .
L OPP	We are one on that subject!
CARL	But you know we're not . . .
L OPP	We agreed . . .
CARL	(*cutting in*) We agreed not to raise the matter. But you did raise the matter. With respect, you raised it just now when you talked as though no one on our side would wish to discuss the republican alternative . . .
L OPP	There is no republican alternative! Don't borrow your language from them! We must have a figurehead in this country that the people can turn to. Someone who offers continuity. Stability. And if you seriously think they'd turn to a president, you can forget it. Without a monarch, the only unifying forces in the country are the Lottery Jackpot and Gary Lineker. And Lineker's had his day. This isn't the time or place . . . make an appointment.

(Jo Benyon *has entered and is observing at a distance.* The Leader of the Opposition *is about to leave him then comes close.*)

I accept that you have never made a secret of your views and I'm sorry if I provoked you without meaning to . . . but to blare the thing out over TV and radio . . . at least don't talk to the press. You know the deadlines. Make yourself scarce.

(*The* Leader of the Opposition *exits. As* Carl *turns he sees* Jo.)

Jo	Interesting intervention.
Carl	(*indicating the party leader*) The boss wasn't too keen.
Jo	You'll be in worse trouble than me.
Carl	I couldn't be in worse trouble than you, Jo. To be a left-winger in the new sanitised, deodorised, decaffeinated Labour Party . . . that really is trouble.
Jo	Are you really anti-monarchy? I never realised.
Carl	It makes sense. The loony left and the rabid right. You don't like them because they're anti-democratic. I don't like them because they're anti-meritocratic. What was your father Jo?
Jo	A printer . . .
Carl	What? In charge?
Jo	What's this? A class contest? He was a craftsman.
Carl	Mine was a farm labourer . . . when he could get work. You were urban working class. I was rural. The lowest! And when I fought my way

	into the boardrooms and got my first chairmanship I received an invite to Buck House . . . a garden party. I didn't go. I wasn't going to shake hands with people who've never done a stroke in their lives.
JO	You'd better be careful. My constituency party's thinking of deselecting me.
CARL	My wife's thinking of deselecting me.
JO	You mean . . . ?
CARL	She's a monarchist. You soon find out who is and who isn't when you start talking this thing for real. If you treat it lightly most will go along with you. They'll even tell you Royal jokes . . . but when they find you're actually serious they're splashing acid. (*A beat.*) We should talk. We both want a debate on the monarchy. Ways and means. We don't have to agree on anything else. We're on a parallel course.
JO	Yes. . . and I have to say I find it pretty disturbing . . .
CARL	Cup of tea?
JO	Oh yes! Taking tea with the far right . . . I'd need a good excuse for that.
CARL	You have one.
JO	Not one I want to reveal yet.
CARL	"Yet". Probably the most significant word in the English language. Well, come on then "yet" me. Or shall I "yet" you? . . . I think we should meet away from here . . .
JO	So do I . . . if it happens. I'll think about it. There's too much at stake winning hearts and minds in my own party without putting it all at risk . . .

CARL	But . . .
JO	Yes. "But" . . . there's always room in my philosophy for the unique event. We need something to push it along.
CARL	How long d'you need to think?
JO	Give me two days. (*She's about to go.*) Here's to the British republic . . .
CARL	The republic!

(*She exits. He watches her go. Sounds of Westminster corridors.*)

Scene Four

A TV studio. The PRINCE'*s interview in progress.* JOHN REESEDALE *sits opposite the* PRINCE. *Out of camera shot are the three persons chosen to take part in an extension of the interview into discussion. But for the moment it is* REESEDALE *and the* PRINCE. *Around them, camera crew, floor manager, quietly going about their business. The* PRINCE *is in mid-comment as the lights rise.*

PRINCE	. . . we must not be over traditionalist or blinkered. Quite frankly, I believe that my family has a lot of catching up to do . . . not to fall behind the vast social changes in modern life. But equally I believe that the nation at large has some catching up to do . . . where changes in the life of the royal family are concerned . . .
JOHN	Could you be specific?
PRINCE	Well everyone's aware that the past thirty years have brought huge increases in divorce . . . both in this country and elsewhere. Divorce is a common part of life. We may regret it . . . or we may feel it avoids much mental torment that was suffered in the past . . . as I think it does.

(He reflects on this for a second.)

On the credit side, there is, of course, more remarriage. But if normal, well-respected people divorce and remarry and if society can take that on board . . . why can't it take on board divorce and remarriage in the royal family?

JOHN
Your father, sir, is not just a normal, well-respected person . . . he is heir to the throne. They expect more.

PRINCE
But you can't just freeze the heir to the throne in the behaviour and moral code of two or three decades ago! You can't preserve him in aspic, just to make people feel that someone up there is toeing the line even if they aren't!

JOHN
Will your father remarry?

PRINCE
I don't know. But if that is his wish I'd be very happy for him . . .

JOHN
Sir . . . will your father renounce the succession?

PRINCE
Slipped in . . . rapier fashion . . . in true, tough questioning style! Of course I'm not going to air his private thinking in public . . . I'd be a poor son if I did . . . so you're not going to hear what passes across the breakfast table.

JOHN
But what do you advise him across the breakfast table?

PRINCE
Advise? I remind him what a loss it would be to this country if such a thing came about.

JOHN
So you do discuss the succession, sir?

PRINCE
We discuss everything. The country would lose a deeply caring man . . . his humanity . . . his patience . . . far more patient than I am. I'm sorry . . . I get angry on his behalf. This

whole succession question . . . it's not just a matter of can we put the crown on the head of a man who has remarried . . . to my father it's a question of 'can I drag the country through what the press would make of that remarriage?' We saw what they made of his marriage to my mother!

(*Again, he pauses for a moment.*)

You see I think I have a right to get angry when you look at the tabloids . . . and not just the tabloids . . . you look at the so-called "respectable" broadsheets. Friend of mine used to say that a tabloid is a paper that always printed the picture of a princess with her slip showing . . . whereas the definition of the respectable papers is those who print a picture of the photographer . . . taking the picture of the princess with her slip showing. The broadsheets have become titillators by proxy. But you could take a poll of all newspaper readers and, even now, you'd have a clear majority in favour of the monarchy . . .

(*He looks to* JOHN *for support.*)

JOHN   Without question, yes . . .

PRINCE   Then why on earth is it that those self-same people carry on buying the paper or magazine when all it is doing is undermining the monarchy by endless intrusions into privacy to find the juicy tit-bit that holds us up to ridicule? Well I think a lot of people should examine themselves on that . . . extraordinary contradiction . . . I hesitate to use a less polite description. They should lie on a couch in a darkened room and think about it!

JOHN   Then . . . sir . . . if your father were to renounce the succession . . . how do you feel about taking on the press?

PRINCE	Sick . . . no. The issue has to be discussed and a solution found. I mean the press used to be more restrained . . . I can't believe it when I look at some of the papers from the fifties. So my father has put up with it for, say, half his life. But I would have to expect to have them in full cry the whole of my life . . . and I intend to live a long time.
JOHN	Are you saying, sir, that you would want a solution *before* you accept the crown?
PRINCE	No, no, no . . . I'd want it to have the highest priority . . . not just for my sake . . . I think it's unhealthy for the nation. But don't ask me what solution.
JOHN	But are you saying you would not accept unless a solution were found?
PRINCE	I'm not making any unilateral statements on that one!
JOHN	Thank you your highness . . . I'd like to move on, if I may, and include the first of our invited guests . . .
	(*There is a break in recording.* JOHN *stands and speaks off camera to the* PRINCE.)
	I thought that went extremely well, sir.
PRINCE	Have we stopped?
	(*A* SOUND MAN *disconnects lapel mikes.*)
JOHN	A very short break, sir. Do stretch your legs if you want to . . . about two minutes . . . so we don't lose the momentum.
PRINCE	What d'you think?
JOHN	I think you're going to change people's perceptions in a remarkable way, sir.
	(*But the* PRINCE *is troubled.*)

PRINCE   I felt I'd started hitting it too hard . . . better rein myself in. Excuse me . . .

(*He says this, seeing* MCNEIL *waiting to pass on a message. He and* MCNEIL *exchange a quiet word.* ELLEN *has entered and takes* JOHN *to one side.*)

ELLEN   They're worried upstairs.

JOHN   They're always worried upstairs. We create programmes. They create neuroses. Once upon a time, in more innocent days, the term 'upstairs' simply meant that which was born up and supported by 'downstairs'. Now, of course, it means that which lives in the permanent, self-inflicted terror of finding that downstairs has slipped out by the back door and is doing something unspeakably subversive . . .

ELLEN   That succession question . . .

JOHN   He was splendid! He matched me! Or was it all too exciting? They don't like that. They want it boring. My dear chap can't you make it more boring? This really doesn't pass the dullness test. Lord preserve us from interesting television!

(*Meanwhile* GWEN *has entered to give the* PRINCE'S *make-up a going over.*)

ELLEN   They've been talking to the palace.

JOHN   Something has to be aired . . . they know it does . . . I'll see them later. No! Nothing must disturb their penthouse dreams of distant knighthoods and sinecurial quangos . . .

(LYDIA WEST *is brought on by the* FLOOR MANAGER. *The* PRINCE *shakes her hand.*)

ELLEN   She's here. I'd better referee.

JOHN	Let them talk.
ELLEN	She might go for him . . .

(ELLEN *goes and has a bright chat with the* PRINCE *as* LYDIA *comes across to* JOHN.)

JOHN	Lydia!
LYDIA	I can't do this!
JOHN	Oh yes you can . . . he's a sweetie!
LYDIA	Well I'm going to come out of it looking all nasty and bitchy and he'll be so nice. He was nice to me just now.
JOHN	Polite but firm . . . same as he is. You'll be fine . . .

(*The* FLOOR MANAGER *makes signs to resume.*)

Sir . . . we'll carry on again, if we may . . .

(*The* PRINCE *crosses to take his seat.* LYDIA *is being wired up.*)

PRINCE	(*to* LYDIA) Don't pull your punches . . .
LYDIA	Well, your highness . . . no, I said that once over there. It's just "sir" from now on isn't it?

(*The* PRINCE *is caught off guard. He'd like to be totally informal but is still a prisoner of family tradition. He spreads his hands in a slightly embarrassed gesture.*)

PRINCE	As you please . . .
LYDIA	Well . . . sir . . . I feel I've been put on the spot . . . I don't really like myself in the role of critic . . .
PRINCE	But that's why we're here . . .
JOHN	Of course it is. Now . . .

LYDIA	Not yet! We don't have to go into it right away, do we?
JOHN	Better we do, yes . . . spontaneity . . . you'll be fine. I'll introduce you . . . lead you in gently . . . it's just an informal conversation . . . Ready?

(FLOOR MANAGER *signals begin. They are now on camera.*)

As I said at the beginning of the programme His Royal Highness wants to meet and talk to critics of the monarchy and here we have a teacher from a junior school in Wolverhampton who made the front pages a few weeks ago when she objected to her children bring taken from class to line the pavements for the recent royal visit . . . Lydia West . . .

LYDIA	No, no . . . I purely felt it should be voluntary. The council seemed to think they should all be paraded and bussed to the city centre and have flags put in their hands . . . I wanted the children to know they could decide about it.
PRINCE	I'm with you all the way. Modern monarchy is by consent. We're not in a totalitarian regime . . .
LYDIA	Maybe . . . sir. But the governors didn't quite see it that way and I was suspended for two days . . . till the parents and the union got it lifted . . .
PRINCE	All I can say is that I'd have done the same in your position.
LYDIA	You mean got yourself suspended?
PRINCE	I assure you, in my family, we have a similar sanction from time to time . . . my brother and I . . . we call it being 'grounded'.

LYDIA	They put my job on the line. They dismissed my professional judgement as though it were worthless!
	(*Awkward pause.* JOHN *comes in smoothly.*)
JOHN	Shall we look at some of the issues here?
LYDIA	(*cutting across*) As though I hadn't even thought about it! No, no . . . hear me out . . . I think . . . sir . . . most people would say I should persuade the children that it's important to obey the laws against racial discrimination . . . and sexual and religious. Now how can I do that and then ask those children to go out and cheer for a family that doesn't keep those laws?
JOHN	I think we should —
LYDIA	Religious . . . take religious. If you, sir, were to marry a Catholic . . . or Muslim . . . or Methodist even . . . you couldn't be king. There's a member of the royal family . . . Prince Michael . . . who married a Catholic . . . so now he's no longer in line . . . he could never succeed to the throne . . .
	(*As* JOHN *is about to interrupt.*)
	Please could I say this out? You take sexual discrimination. If you, sir, had an older sister you would still be heir to the throne ahead of her. Your younger brother is next in line after you . . . but if there had been a sister in between she would be ignored and passed over in favour of him. The queen only reigns because she didn't have a brother! Princess Anne who many would like to succeed her is way down the list because she's female! It's unbelievable! No . . . no . . . I'm sorry I have to complete this . . . racial discrimination . . . there has been a law against it since nineteen seventy-something. And yet at the time the law went through parliament they make an

exception in the case of the Royal household
. . . and it was a Labour Government who did
it. I've sometimes thought when you watch the
procession down the Mall . . . where are the
black faces under those powdered wigs? Where
are the turbans? Where's the black coachman?
No, please . . . I didn't want to go on like this
. . . I didn't want to be here! I really let myself
be talked into it because there's one thing I
have to say. When the council said they were
sending round busses to take the children to
wave their flags . . . I thought: yes! They'll
send transport for that! Our kid's parents are
some of the poorest in the area. We've gone
on our knees for busses to take them to a
nature reserve or a Christmas play . . . but this
. . . no problem! And you, sir . . . I'm sorry sir
. . . you just belong to a different world from
them . . . you have millions! There's hardly
any family anywhere as rich as yours. How can
you have the remotest inkling of the losing
battle some of my children will be condemned
to? They have nothing! How can I have
respect for a family sitting on all that wealth
. . . most of it ours . . . and expecting those
children to come out and cheer for them?

(*She breaks off, trembling. The* PRINCE *is
silent, staring at her, appalled by the pent up
antagonism in her.* JOHN *and the* FLOOR
MANAGER *make signs that the tape is no longer
running.*)

JOHN   Have some water. These studios can be very
oppressive. Maybe you'd like to take a rest.
We'll come back to later . . . (*The lights fade
as he gently speaks to her, the* PRINCE *unable
to take his eyes from her.*) Then we'll go over
the same ground but make it more of a two-
way dialogue . . . throw the thoughts around a
bit . . .

(*Fade to black.*)

Scene Five

Westminster. Defence questions, following on from PM's question time. KERRIGAN-LARBY *is on his feet.*

KERRIGAN-LARBY The question I ask the right honourable lady, Mr Deputy Speaker, is perfectly simple. This European navy . . . how would the components of such a notley fleet actually communicate? Would there be a common language? Would that language be English . . . and if not, why not?

(*The* JUNIOR DEFENCE MINISTER *rises from the labour front bench.*)

MINISTER All matters to do with the Combined European Naval Task Force, including communications, are still under discussion, Mr Deputy Speaker.

KERRIGAN-LARBY Beacuse the French and Spanish are still objecting to English! And if they get their way, the Germans and Italians will make trouble until we end up with orders being given in a dozen languages! Is this navy to be a cross between a ship of fools and a tower of Babel?

GIERSON If it's any help, Mr Deputy Speaker, the Spanish for "Hello Sailor" is "Hola, Marinere!" . . . I don't know the French . . .

(*Fade to black.*)

Scene Six

The living room of CARL POINTER'S *London flat. Basically, two chairs and a TV console.*

CARL *is watching a section of the* PRINCE'S *interview that we've seen being recorded. We hear the* PRINCE'S *voice without necessarily seeing him on the screen.*

CARL's *wife* SARAH *joins him and looks at the TV over his shoulder.*

CARL — Watch this bit . . . watch his eyes!

(*He is gleeful at what he sees as the* PRINCE'S *uncertainty. She is contemptuous of her husband's air of triumph. He leaps to the video and winds back slightly . . . replaying the previous fifteen seconds.*)

Watch again! (*Winds back, plays.*) See? He's wavering! He's on the edge!

(*She reacts scornfully. The door bell rings. He switches off. She goes to the door, offstage.*)

SARAH — I'll let her in.

(*She admits* JO BENYON.)

Hello. You're Jo Benyon. Sarah Pointer. We met once at the House . . . Speaker's tea party . . .

JO — Oh I remember very well . . .

SARAH — You thought: who's this Tory bitch?

JO — No I didn't. I'm sorry haring round like this . . . am I putting you out?

SARAH — No, no. The lion's in his den . . . and very pleased with himself.

CARL — See the prince?

JO — It's why I'm here . . .

CARL — You said you'd only meet me on neutral ground.

JO — I got the taxi to drop me in the next street and made sure nobody saw me coming in . . .

SARAH — You're not serious?

Jo	No.
Sarah	I grew up in a house where guests of every political hue were constantly invited. I always think curiosity is more interesting than prejudice . . . but now we live in such stupidly divided times . . .
Jo	You might not think that if you were a backbencher in the "new" Labour Party. You might think they weren't divided enough.
Sarah	Ah . . . would you call yourself a Marxist?
Jo	I used to have a short reply to that but now it's crept into four volumes . . .
Sarah	Well, we have enough division here. You see, I'm not of his persuasion. I'm not one of the hi-tech lunatic fringe of the party who believe that all the nation's ills can be cured by universal deregulation and wiring everyone up to the informational super-highway. I'm a Conservative in the traditional mould, as my father was . . .
Carl	Village squire-ish . . . soft-ish, liberal-ish . . . shake hands but mentally touch your forelock. As a peasant yokel I couldn't escape the ambition to marry into the country set. Once I made my money I had to see if you could buy them.
Sarah	My father was one of those long gone Conservatives who actually believed in conserving things . . . which Carl thinks is terribly quaint. Carl's in a category of his own because of this monarchy thing . . . but otherwise a standard new Tory. They're like the new Beaujolais . . . the freshness soon turns to vinegar and they have to be left a few years to mature.

(Jo *is embarrassed by the edge to the exchanges.*)

JO I have called at a bad time . . .

CARL Not at all. Share some of this . . . we're celebrating . . .

(*Gets champagne.*)

JO What?

CARL We're getting divorced.

SARAH Our separation. We part tomorrow. Then we plan the divorce. I'm sure Jo doesn't want to hear this. Please don't feel embarrassed . . . it's not personal. Entirely a matter of principle. We're politically incompatible. No . . . I got over my personal revulsion for him years ago . . . didn't I dearest?

CARL Certainly did, doll . . .

(*He plies* JO *with champagne and* SARAH *hands her the nuts, etc.*)

SARAH So . . . you saw His Royal Highness . . .

CARL He was wavering . . .

JO On the edge . . .

CARL My words! Just now!

(*He appeals to* SARAH, *who is scornful.*)

SARAH Yes, well . . . I'll let you talk. I have to get ready for a council meeting . . . trying to get true conservatism back on the rails after his lot hijacked the train. Remember you have a guest in the next room . . . (*To* JO.) We must meet properly one of these days. I'll see you as I go out.

(*She exits.*)

JO A guest . . . ?

CARL	He's making a few calls . . . he won't interrupt us. What brings you?
JO	The moment the programme was over I had the Lib-Dems on . . . Alan Greerson . . . they want to form an all-party group . . . a republican group . . .
CARL	To do what?
JO	Work towards a full debate in the House and a committee . . . I mean, I assume you can't exactly have a Royal Commission to examine republicanism. They also want us to appear as a cross-party group in the national campaign for an end to the monarchy.
CARL	Wish it had been you and not them . . .
JO	What does it matter? They were the first to discuss it at their party conference . . . when we were afraid to . . .
CARL	Look . . . you've got forty-upwards you can count on. Lib-Dems have, say, half a dozen. In my case there is just me . . . and maybe two others . . . I'm out on the . . . slimmest of limbs . . . and I like it . . . but, numbers aside, we should rotate the chairmanship of the group . . . yourself, Alan and me.
JO	Mine wouldn't wear it. Sorry. And you're forgetting the Scot-Nats and others. You're too controversial . . . and, as you say, you've got no troops.
CARL	But I do have access to money.
JO	Much?
CARL	Oh yes.
JO	Where from?
CARL	It's sitting next door. Sir James Heaney.

(She looks inquiringly.)

Heaney? No? Come on, Jo. You drive up the motorway. You see it on trucks and bulldozers . . .

JO Ah, yes . . .

CARL The construction company. Jim Heaney has millions, Jo . . . and he wants to put some of them into the republican campaign.

JO Why?

CARL He'd best tell you himself . . . look, this isn't set up. He contacted me because he wasn't sure how you'd receive him. He came over to watch the Prince's show with us, then when you rang he thought he'd stay on. You're the one he needs to meet . . .

JO What are his motives?

CARL He's non-party. His company hasn't paid into Tory funds for the past twenty years. If anything he's SDP . . . which really makes him one of you . . .

(Jo deflects the jibe with a warning gesture.)

JO Don't!

CARL Talk to him. We'll have dinner. You won't be seen. We'll eat here. It's a service flat. I only have to ring . . .

(He takes her silence as agreement and exits to another room.)

(off) Jim . . . come and meet her.

(CARL re-enters with SIR JAMES HEANEY, a smiling, almost saintly man in his seventies.)

JAMES How very wonderful . . . how really delightful! I have been sitting in there like a bridesmaid at a wedding . . . hoping someone would throw

	me a bouquet . . . and here we are. Touching hands . . .
Jo	He's told me you want to contribute to the republican campaign. Why is that?
James	To the point. To the point. Firstly, I'd say, because I'm a republican in my soul . . . I'm an Irishman . . . though my person, as opposed to my soul, is British. I've lived here . . . made my money here . . . married here . . . have British nationality. I married a girl from Hertfordshire, who turned out to be so much of an angel that they decided up there that they wanted her back. I'm alone . . . I have an abundance of means but not an abundance of time . . .

(*During this* SARAH *has re-entered, ready to go to her meeting.*)

	I want to do something for my adopted country.
Sarah	By undermining its institutions?
James	I would say by renewing them. Britain to me is like one of those immemorial trees, admired for its strength and its beauty . . . for its great age and abundant foliage . . . until people think back and realize that it seems to put out a few less . . . and a few less leaves each year. They investigate and find it's because it's gone hollow inside.
Sarah	I must go to my meeting . . . but I don't agree. No. No! The tree is putting out less leaves because of the inadequate attentions of the Downing Street tree surgeons. The tree is sound at the centre . . . and solid! This is ridiculous . . . you don't so much argue with Sir James as wallow in his metaphors. What I do say is . . . (*She fights a surge of emotion.*) . . . if this country ever loses its monarchy I'll live abroad.

CARL: Where? Denmark? Holland? Belgium? Spain? Monaco?

SARAH: It's the monarchies in Europe that are the best places to live . . .

CARL: They're the hangers on! Monaco lives off France . . . Denmark, Holland and Belgium live off Germany . . . and Spain lives off our fish!

SARAH: I'm going to have the last word because, like Nora in the Doll's House . . . I'm going to go out and slam the door. To me our monarchy is what gives our country a human face and a feeling of warmth and continuity . . . way above the cockpit of Westminster! If you want to replace her with some shifty superannuated politician then you'd better think how you define yourselves as human beings . . . because you have ice in your veins!

(*She exits.* CARL *holds up a finger.*)

CARL: Listen.

(*We hear a door slam.*)

Now . . . carry on. If we're all feeling warm enough . . .

JO: (*to* SIR JAMES) Are there any conditions attached to this money you want to give?

JAMES: That it should be all-party. And I think I should not be seen to be the only donor. I think funds should come from as many quarters as possible . . .

JO: Don't you think it will seem a contradiction that you want to be part of a republican movement? You have a knighthood. The queen gave it you . . .

JAMES	You know, I was infatuated by her. Her smile is the most difficult argument we have to face. I felt the tip of the sword on my shoulders . . . light as a bird . . . a blue-eyed bird. Well . . . I shall resign the knighthood. Sad but necessary . . . and while we're about it we'll make some publicity out of it. This movement will be no movement at all unless a good many people who are now royalist have a change of heart. In a sense they'll all be giving up their knighthoods.
JO	I'm still not seeing your motive.
JAMES	I'll give you a personal motive . . . and a public one. For me, loving Britain and Ireland, it has been painful all my life to endure the rift between them . . . or between violent interests there and here . . . while all the time the people have so much to give each other. Over there the queen is called "the English Queen". The monarchy is the obstacle to the healing process. But as two republics, side by side, we could bury the sins of the fathers and be what we should be . . . close cousins in a brilliant family. I want the south to come back into the union — a very different kind of union — then I'll die a happy man.
JO	But what about Ulster?
CARL	A detail! You're dealing with a visionary and like all visionaries he can see with eyes closed but not with them open.
JAMES	We have just given Ulster its own devolved government. It's half way to having its own republic! People say if the monarchy is weakened the United Kingdom will break up. But I think the monarchy is one of the causes of the break up because no matter how they pretend to be Scots or Welsh, they inevitably represent the domination by England. A republic is the only hope of keeping the thing

	together. (*To* Jo.) But tell me, why are you for a republic?
JO	Because I believe the government should be the people's government and not her majesty's.
JAMES	And that will make them feel better?
JO	It's not a matter of how they feel. If laws are made in the name of the people and not her majesty then there is a gain in direct democratic power . . . even if it's only the power to see into government and lift the fusty curtain of secrecy that's there in the name of the crown. There's too much temptation for the government to take on the style of monarchy and treat the people like its subjects.
JAMES	No more subservience?
JO	Exactly. The people should be citizens and not subjects . . . with a citizen president as Head of State.
CARL	Trouble with being a member of Parliament is that you're too often on your feet uttering while nobody's listening because they're busy composing in their heads what they want to utter. This is the real world, Jo. What does "no more subservience" mean?
JO	He said it, not me . . . and don't bore me by pretending not to know . . .
CARL	In a republic, people will still have bosses to work for and clients they want to keep . . .
JO	And can't it be done without subservience?
CARL	There has to be a chain of command. Management has to manage . . .
JO	To pocket the profits.

CARL	There has to be profit.
JO	Whatever it costs?
JAMES	Carl . . . why do you want a republic?
CARL	To make Britain a leader instead of a follower. To make it a more efficient machine for living in . . . working in . . . and making money in . . . and I mean everybody. I'm against royalty for the same reasons as the editor of the Economist . . . because they're anti-capitalist. Catch them putting their sons or daughters into the City or industry . . . unless it's some joke job in the arts. Bloody hell! Can we expect two hard-driving republics like France or Germany to take us seriously . . . when every now and then we still have to indulge in some mystic orgy of trailing velvet and ermine and jewel-encrusted totems across the hallowed floors of Westminster Abbey in the wake of silver stick?
JAMES	Not surprisingly, where I connect with both of you, it's from two different directions. Let me give you my public reason now. Carl, as a Conservative, have you read Disraeli's "Sybil . . . or the Two Nations?"
CARL	Nobody has. Correction . . . my wife has. I died somewhere on page five.
JAMES	Jo?
JO	(*guarded*) I've looked at it. Didn't he say that the whole aim of politics was to bring justice to the people?
	(*She glances at* CARL, *who ripostes.*)
CARL	Not, you'll notice, for the people to bring justice to themselves . . .
JAMES	Please . . . it was something else he said that also caught my imagination. I've always identified with Disraeli as an outsider

observing the English . . . he a Jew . . . I an Irishman. He said you can never fully understand the English unless you see them as a conquered nation. He meant literally conquered . . . by William of Normandy a thousand years ago. When he gave every town, village, farm and field in England to his followers, the English became a defeated people . . . the Normans stole the land, levied swingeing rents and taxes and put their monarchs on the throne. Now, as Disraeli said . . . they're still there. Even in our time! Still there, enmeshed into the nation. The land-owning gentry of England . . . either direct descendants of Normans or those who bought the stolen loot from them . . . still there! And at their centre, the chief landowner, the queen. And down the centuries, forced to be slaves to the land or industry . . . or dead slaves on the fields of Paschendale and the Somme . . . this same defeated people has never . . . despite all the apparent political advances . . . has never quite been able to take back what was stolen by those who first set foot on the shingle at Hastings.

JO (*to* SIR JAMES) Are *you* a Marxist?

JAMES You might as well ask "am I a beached whale". No. What I want a republic to give back to that defeated people is what has always been denied them . . . a sense of liberty . . . not just in here . . . (*He puts his hand on his heart.*) . . . but in here.

(*He taps his forehead.* CARL *considers, then takes the phone.*)

CARL (*on phone*) Restaurant . . .

(*With his free hand he passes them menus. Speaks to them as he waits to he put through.*)

Avoid the smoked eel. The hors d'oeuvre's good.

(*Fade to black.*)

Scene Seven

A country estate. A pheasant shoot, the shooting party in position, waiting, guns and loaders. The PRINCE *is well in evidence, eyes fixed ahead of him. Silence.*

Then we hear the beaters approaching, calling sharply, whistling, striking with their sticks.

Suddenly a commotion as the birds take to the air and the firing begins . . . one barrel, two barrels . . . loader hands another gun and reloads. Shooters follow birds around in flight, working fast.

Quickly it's all over. One gun . . . another . . . silence. During this, the PRINCE'S *young brother has arrived. We'll call him by his nickname,* SKIP. *He watches, trying to keep up an air of enjoyment, but inwardly tense. He is in his turn watched by the ever-present* MCNEIL.

The PRINCE *has a quick, self-deprecating word with his loader, then sees* SKIP.

PRINCE   Well that was quite a performance . . . I don't think I've ever done worse. (*To* SKIP.) Don't say you were watching that?

SKIP   Not all of it . . .

PRINCE   I was awful! Too high and fast for me. And then . . . I wasn't concentrating.

         (*He reads the look on* SKIP'S *face.*)

         Is it news?

         (SKIP *nods.*)

         Father?

SKIP	Yes. It's all tied up . . . He's decided.
	(*He produces a letter.*)
PRINCE	When?
SKIP	Didn't say. He wants you to know first.
PRINCE	Look . . . we're brothers. I won't have differences made. What I have to face you could have to face.
SKIP	Three days time.
	(*The* PRINCE *opens and reads the letter.*)
PRINCE	So soon . . . and I thought he might change his mind.
	(*Hands letter to* SKIP, *who reads it.* LADY CONSTANCE *enters, having been with the shooting party which is now wandering away.*)
	Hello Connie!
CONNIE	How many?
PRINCE	Didn't count.
CONNIE	I'll ask your loader.
PRINCE	Don't ask him, he's too honest. I tell you there were two or three elderly woodcock who were sorry they met up with me.
	(CONNIE *is obviously smitten.*)
CONNIE	Cool! I was brilliant, of course . . . thank you for asking . . . and I'm starving . . . lunching?
PRINCE	I'll be along. Got a bit of brother talk first.
CONNIE	(*sensing what it is*) Oh no! I'll leave you. I'm so sorry. It's all such an awful shame. God how I hate all this hounding that's going on!
PRINCE	See you in a moment.

(LADY CONSTANCE *exits.* SKIP *hands back the letter.*)

SKIP: I ought to say congratulations or something more high sounding if I could think of it. It's one of our "what-ifs", isn't it? What if you became heir apparent. Now you are.

(*He says it feeling out his brother's reaction.*)

PRINCE: The poison chalice . . .

SKIP: (*fighting down his emotions*) No! Come on!

(*They're alone except for* MCNEIL. *The* PRINCE *notes him trying to look as though he's not trying to eavesdrop.*)

I've never heard him talk about you like he did. He keeps saying you're much more worth it than he is.

PRINCE: (*to* MCNEIL) Got a note pad?

(MCNEIL *gets out a note pad and biro and leans so that the* PRINCE *can write using his back to rest the pad on.*)

We're leaving.

MCNEIL: When sir?

PRINCE: Five minutes. I'll do this apology for Lord Radcliff . . . would you take it for me . . . and when you pass Lady Constance on the way tell her I've had to go. Say I'm sorry.

(MCNEIL *takes the message.*)

MCNEIL: Where are we going sir?

PRINCE: Home.

(MCNEIL *exits. The* PRINCE *takes a good look at the landscape.*)

	I want to remember where I was when it happened.
SKIP	I'll remind you.
PRINCE	Stunning piece of countryside. Look at those hills! But is it the most appropriate place to be told this, I wonder.
SKIP	What? Knee deep in dead birds?
PRINCE	Should have been in the rain on a building site at some dreary foundation stone gig.
SKIP	Can't help the weather.
PRINCE	We ask ourselves two questions. Can doing this job be beneficial to anyone when all we are is joke fodder for every newspaper and TV stand-up comic? And secondly, is it humanly possible to do it now that it's open season on our private lives? Alright, there are other issues . . . deeper issues. . . but these are the ones where the flames have got too close . . .
SKIP	Don't ask me to answer . . . but I made up my mind coming along . . . whatever you decide. I mean whatever . . . it's up to me to back you right down the line.
PRINCE	Only you and I know what it's like . . . it's that old exclusive club of two again. Skip . . . I've got to think. I need four or five days away.
SKIP	Well take them.
PRINCE	Not just "away." Away from myself. Away from "it" and what I am to others. Somewhere there's some truth about this . . . and it lies in the answer to that other question, do they really want us?
SKIP	Ah . . . but that's a fact, isn't it? Most do.

PRINCE	But I want to know why. Is it for the crowns and swords and plumes and honours . . . all the props from some pantomime that closed years ago? Or is it the modern version . . . the Royal soap opera where no one ever seems to get written out?
SKIP	I don't think it's for anything that much . . . just wanting things to carry on.
PRINCE	Oh yes I can quite see why one's friends want us. Lord Radcliff there . . . all these people . . . Connie. It's the golden life and we're a kind of flux to keep it flowing. But if you had nothing. Nothing. What possible reason could you have for wanting things to carry on? Yet I think it's as you say . . . incredibly, they want us! But why should they? I've never met anyone with nothing . . . or, if I have, I didn't know it.
SKIP	What are you going to do? I mean, if you renounce it too . . .
PRINCE	I just need to be clear . . .
SKIP	But if you turn it down, that goes for me as well. I won't take your place . . .
PRINCE	Let's take the jumps as they come.
SKIP	But I won't take your place . . .
PRINCE	You don't have to promise anything.
SKIP	(*still insisting*) I won't!
PRINCE	This is simply for peace of mind and soul. I need to talk to people . . . I mean, one to one. I have this brain-splitting sensation on just being able to go up to someone in the street and talk to them . . . yet if they know who I am it kills it stone dead.
SKIP	You should use the Internet. Talk to people on the computer. No . . . you can do it

	anonymously now. There's an agency in Finland that puts your message out under a code name and gets the replies back . . .
PRINCE	Yes, that's good isn't it? I start off trying to reach people who have nothing and end up talking exclusively to Internet freaks with PCs and modems! (*Pause*.) Remember when we were kids we used to take turns to tell stories after lights out . . . and we kept telling the same story in different versions . . .
SKIP	"Getting over the wire."
PRINCE	That one. Getting free. Walking the streets. Trouble is we've been brought up differently, you and I. We've seen too much beyond the gates. Will you help me?
SKIP	How?
PRINCE	We're at Wembley Stadium at the weekend . . .
SKIP	Won't it be cancelled?
PRINCE	It's the Toyota Cup Millennium Match . . .
SKIP	I mean you and me going.
PRINCE	It's our first job after the renunciation. I think it's important we are there.
SKIP	But if you want to get away . . .
PRINCE	That's not so easy, is it? I shouldn't ask this. Will you help me?
SKIP	How?
PRINCE	We go to Wembley. Watch the match. Do the ceremony. Then we've got the reception . . . half an hour . . . then two hour's drive to Gloucestershire for dinner. I've asked for a changing room at Wembley so we can dress before we start out.
SKIP	Why? We can do that at the other end.

PRINCE	No. Wembley.
	(*His firmness makes* SKIP *realise.*)
SKIP	What are you going to do?
PRINCE	Get over the wire . . .
	(*The* PRINCE *has his eye on* MCNEIL *returning.* MCNEIL *enters. He's well aware that he has put a stop on their conversation. He hands the* PRINCE *a note.*)
MCNEIL	From his lordship, sir . . . and Lady Constance says she quite understands.
PRINCE	Thank you.
	(*Fade to black.*)

Scene Eight

House of Commons debating chamber. The scattering of members will rapidly be increased as others arrive to hear the expected Prime Ministerial statement. The PM, *however, is not yet in place.*

The TORY OPPOSITION LEADER *is on his feet, concluding a speech.*

L OPP	. . . and now let me remind the House that my position here . . . my role . . . which I consider a great privilege, is that of leader of *Her Majesty's* Loyal Opposition. And the right honourable ladies and gentlemen opposite are members of a government which is *Her Majesty's* Loyal Government . . .
GIERSON	And Parliament's the people's!
L OPP	Of course it's the people's! But the people are content that it is held, so to speak, in trust for them by the monarch . . . so that when the queen says, "My Parliament", this is what she

	means . . . hers on behalf of her people. Madam Speaker, when the Prime Minister arrives shortly and tells us what he may have to tell us . . .
	(*Cries of "He knows . . . he knows!"*)
SPEAKER	Order! Let's not waste the few minutes we have in hand . . .
L OPP	Whatever is said, I want this House to reflect on it's loyalty to the Crown . . . something which we on this side take very seriously.
	(GIERSON *indicates* CARL POINTER.)
GIERSON	With exceptions!
	(*Laughter.* CARL POINTER *makes a small gesture of acknowledgement. The* LEADER OF THE OPPOSITION *is inwardly furious.*)
L OPP	The queen . . . the sovereign . . . is the secure hub of our state . . . the ever-stabilising presence in our political life . . . and, as head of the Church, an inspiration in our spiritual life. Let the party opposite repudiate those who try to sweep aside a loyalty, Madam Speaker, that I regard as a gift from God . . . which should be as natural to us as the air we breathe . . .
	(*A roar of approval from the Tory benches.* JO BENYON *is on her feet.*)
JO	Is it in order, Madam Speaker, for the right honourable gentleman to question the loyalty of members like myself who seek to examine the case against monarchy . . . openly, in debate? Is he implying that there are subjects which are taboo in this House? Is the queen disloyal to accept republics within the Commonwealth? Is *he* disloyal by not calling for Britain's withdrawal from Europe when

Europe itself is clearly republic in character? It has *presidents* of its council commission and assembly . . . and, down the road, if ever there were need for a head of the European Superstate . . . is anyone ready to suggest a king or queen of Europe? I doubt it! Shouldn't he rather be rescuing our queen from a Europe where she has no real place and about as much significance as the Dame of Sark?

(*Laughter. Boos.* CARL POINTER *rises sardonically.*)

CARL: I find that an offensive remark, Madam Speaker.

SPEAKER: I agree, Mr Pointer . . . though I'm surprised you do.

CARL: Madam . . . I think that the onus is on republicans to behave better than monarchists . . . after all, we do have all the arguments on our side.

SPEAKER: I'm sure the honourable lady doesn't wish to spoil her case . . . I invite her to withdraw the remark.

(JO, *amused by* CARL'S *intervention, smiles graciously.*)

JO: You are wise as always, Madam Speaker, I withdraw it. In place of it I'll say that the position of the queen in Europe would be as unenviable as the position of a pro-republican backbencher in the loyal party opposite.

(JO *sits. A Tory* (KERRIGAN-LARBY) *rises.*)

SPEAKER: Is it important, Mr Kerrigan-Larby?

KERRIGAN-LARBY: Yes Madam Speaker.

SPEAKER	And brief?
KERRIGAN-LARBY	Yes Madam. I would like to correct a scurrilous article in today's Guardian about the export of British ball bearings to Abu Dhabi . . .

(*But the* PM *has entered. A serious look on his face.*)

SPEAKER	We were out of time, Mr Kerrigan-Larby. You'll have an opportunity later. Prime Minister's statement!

(*The* PM *rises. He has a letter in a leather-bound folder.*)

PM	Madam Speaker, events have overtaken us and I'm afraid this will not be the statement I was to make. I have to inform you that a message from the Prince of Wales to this House was received a short time ago, signed by his own hand and addressed to us all. I ask you, Madam Speaker, to make the contents known.

(*He hands on the folder to* MADAM SPEAKER.)

SPEAKER	Right honourable and honourable members, His Royal Highness writes as follows. (*Reads.*) "After long and serious consideration, I have determined to renounce my succession to the throne. I take this action because I am convinced that it is in the best interests of the kingdom, of the continuance of good government, and the future happiness of the British people. I have, therefore, caused to be executed an instrument of renunciation and desire that effect should be given to it immediately."

(*A slow fade to black, as we hear the roar of the crowd at Wembley.*)

Scene Nine

A Director/VIP's changing room, Wembley Stadium. We hear the crowd reaction to the presentation ceremony. This obviously, can't identify the winning team.

The sound should mix into crowd beginning to leave, brass band playing them out, etc.

During this McNeil *enters and does a final security check, just as he did in the TV make up room in Scene One. He listens to the crowd a moment, then dials a number on his mobile.*

McNeil   Don't go to sleep out there . . . I'm in the VIP's changing room . . . they'll be here any moment. I'd say fifteen to twenty minutes . . . I'll give you the word . . . you know which exit? . . . Yes, that one. Don't move till I say or we'll have a crowd round the car . . .

(*Enter a* Director of Wembley Stadium *ushering in the* Prince *and* Skip. *Other officials and security staff could crowd in the doorway.*)

Director   . . . I do hope you'll find everything you require, your highness . . .

Prince   I'm sure we will. Thank you.

director   We've arranged for you to leave by a quiet side exit, sir, so you won't be spotted, as it were . . .

McNeil   I've asked Rogers not to bring the car round till the last moment, sir. . .

Prince   Good. We're really most grateful to you and your staff.

Director   Oh you've done us an honour, your highnesses, you truly have. We all realise what a difficult time this is for you, sir. . . for you both. And for you to allow yourselves to be here at all was quite magnificent. The game

	needs its higher moments . . . its moments of grace.
PRINCE	Well you had them today . . . a pleasure to watch. Open and stylish.
SKIP	That last corner!
PRINCE	Tremendous . . . absolute blinder!
DIRECTOR	I'm glad you enjoyed it, your highnesses. What I'm saying is that occasions like this help remove some of the stains that we're all aware of on the game's reputation . . . and put us back, you might say, in a clean strip.
PRINCE	Very much so. And that's what we're here to do.

(*The* DIRECTOR *looks momentarily puzzled. The* PRINCE *indicates the changing room.*)

Get into clean strip.

(*Laughter. The* DIRECTOR *bows, knowing his presence is no longer required.*)

DIRECTOR	A pleasant journey, your highnesses . . . and I hope you'll be our guests on many more occasions.
PRINCE	I'm sure we will be . . .

(*Handshakes. The* DIRECTOR *departs.* MCNEIL *ushers everyone away from the door and is about to close it with himself still in the room.*)

PRINCE	I think we'll be alright . . .

(*He is excluding* MCNEIL, *who is well aware of it.*)

MCNEIL	I thought you might need some help, sir . . . with no valet here.
PRINCE	Thank you . . . but we have been known to change our clothes unassisted. Actually . . . we need to talk.

MCNEIL	I'll be in the corridor, sir.
	(*He exits, closing the door.* SKIP *quietly re-opens it a crack and peers out.*)
SKIP	He's at the top of the stairs.
PRINCE	Alone?
SKIP	Yes.
PRINCE	Anyone to the left?
	(SKIP *strains to look the other way without being seen.*)
SKIP	No, it's a dead end.
PRINCE	So the security men are at the bottom of the stairs by the exit . . .
SKIP	Right.
	(*A fractional pause while both search one another's faces, trying to think of anything they may not have anticipated . . . then they move into action.*)
PRINCE	Turn the showers on in there.
	(SKIP *exits to do so. We hear a hiss of water to make it seem as though they're showering. They take off their suits and shirts. The* PRINCE *has well-worn jeans under his trousers and a stained T-shirt under his shirt.* SKIP *has a thin old sweater under his shirt. He removes it and the* PRINCE *slips it over his T-shirt. From the two cases they produce toilet bags. In one is a pair of worn trainers . . . in the other a tightly rolled up thin bomber jacket and a baseball-type cap. The* PRINCE *gets all the clothes on while* SKIP *now gets himself into one of the dinner suits. The* PRINCE *sniffs the bomber jacket.*)

PRINCE	Stinks! You'd think Sandringham'd have a better class of jumble . . . (*Sees name on inside of jacket.*) Who's PJW?
SKIP	Dunno . . .
PRINCE	I thought I'd be SC.
SKIP	Who's that?
PRINCE	Stuart Charles. It's Charles Stuart backwards.

(SKIP *pulls a face.*)

Bonny Prince Charlie, He went in disguise . . . sailed to Skye dressed as a woman.

SKIP	Not Stuart . . . you ought to be Kev or Wayne.
PRINCE	Look in the cupboard . . . see if there's a sponge mop or something I can use as a prop.

(SKIP, *still wrestling his things on, looks. While he does so, the* PRINCE *produces a jar of hair grease and flattens his hair. Rubs a pale cream on his face . . . sticks a ready-cut bit of plaster over one eye and clips an earring in one ear.* SKIP *finds a steward's fluorescent bib in the bottom of the cupboard.*)

SKIP	No mops or buckets. One of these . . .
PRINCE	Good. Anything else?
SKIP	Box of light bulbs and steps . . . you could be the maintenance man. If you're spotted, climb up and change a bulb . . .

(*But the* PRINCE *has stopped . . . uncertain.*)

PRINCE	I can't do it.
SKIP	What? Change a light bulb?
PRINCE	I can't involve you!
SKIP	You've got to involve me . . .

PRINCE	It's ridiculous! Irresponsible.
SKIP	Don't waver. I'm helping you.
PRINCE	No!
SKIP	We're in now. This is the most fun I've ever had. Back of your neck . . . (*He helps put more pale cream on his brother's neck.*) This looks awful!
PRINCE	It covers the tan. The unemployed don't have tans!
SKIP	Well you do and according to Private Eye you're unemployed.
PRINCE	How's the face?
SKIP	What about the moustache?
PRINCE	No. It looks false . . .
SKIP	It looked good . . .
PRINCE	It felt wrong . . . no. Now . . . the letters . . . (*Produces a file of letters from the bag.*) All labelled. This explains my reasons to everybody and sums up my views. (*Shows two more.*) Father, mother. (*Another letter.*) This for McNeil's inspector absolving him from blame . . . (*He takes the whole file and props it up on a bench.*) I'll leave it propped up here.)
SKIP	Now I'm worrying . . . God this is dangerous. It's not Windsor Park out there.
PRINCE	It's where people live their lives, Skip. And I can't deny it. As far as I'm concerned it's a foreign country . . . and I'm supposed to be its future king!
SKIP	If someone realises . . .
PRINCE	(*east London accent*) Nah . . . they ain't gonna tumble this. No fucker's gonna tumble

	this, mate. (*In normal voice.*) That reminds me . . . I recorded a chunk off EastEnders . . .
	(*He gets a walkman from the bag and slips it in the pocket of the bomber jacket. He switches it on. Listens. Switches it off and repeats a phrase in an East End accent.*)
	"Leave it aht, will yer? You done enuff aggro fer one day. Point taken? Know what I mean?"
Skip	(*corrects his accent*) "Leave it aht!"
Prince	(*practising*) "Leave it aht!"
	(*A tap on the door. We hear* McNeil.)
McNeil	(*off*) Excuse me sir, shall I order the car up?
	(*They glance at one another.*)
Prince	(*whispers*) In the shower.
	(Skip *opens the door slightly. The* Prince *gets out of sight.* Skip *is in dinner jacket by now, bow tie to be tied.*)
Skip	Give it five minutes, sergeant. He's still in the shower.
McNeil	(*off*) Fine, sir.
	(Skip *watches* McNeil *as he goes back to his position outside. He closes the door.*)
Prince	Wet the shirt . . .
	(Skip *takes the* Prince's *dress shirt from the hanger and exits to showers. He returns with the shirt soaking wet.*)
Skip	Wet enough?
Prince	You take it to McNeil and you say . . .
Skip	I say, "He's dropped this in the shower. He thinks there should be another one in the valise in the car." Is there?

PRINCE	How should I know? Richards packed it. Now . . . you stay at the top of the stairs as though you're keeping watch for him. He goes down with it because he can't ask Rogers to leave the car . . . and he's not going to hand HRH's shirt to some gash security man. Once he's out of view . . .
SKIP	I come back and tap twice.
PRINCE	I exit. Keep walking. Past you. Past the stairs. Right round to the other side. Out . . . and I'm with the homegoers. With the crowd . . .
SKIP	You're bound to meet security . . .
PRINCE	(*east London*) Then I'll have to use me wits won't I sunshine? (*Back to own accent.*) When I pass you?
SKIP	I go down the stairs as though I've not bothered to keep watch . . . when McNeil comes back I tell him the joke about the Titanic . . . talk about the match . . . delay him while you get to the street. Is this going to work?
PRINCE	Of course it's going to work. But let McNeil get ahead of you and come into the room first. He finds it empty . . . notes of explanation left, etc . . . you had no idea I was about to do this.
SKIP	I'm not so sure I'm not going to tell them.
PRINCE	At least you don't know where I'll be.
SKIP	I wonder what they'll do?
PRINCE	I don't know. I rather think they won't rush to make it public. It's important to do this. Tell me it's important.
SKIP	If you have to declare . . . then it's you who has to find out. It's what you said.

PRINCE	Yes.
	(*The moment has come.*)
SKIP	Did Charlie Stuart get recognised?
PRINCE	Not sure. Richard the First didn't. Nor Henry the Fifth.
SKIP	King Alfred was assaulted for burning the cakes.
PRINCE	I won't burn any cakes.
SKIP	Your electronic tag?
PRINCE	Stays here . . . McNeil attached it to the dinner jacket. Go!
	(SKIP *exits, taking the wet shirt. The* PRINCE *checks his face in the mirror. Jams the hat down. Puts the steward's "bib" on . . . then as an afterthought takes the aluminium steps from the cupboard, puts his arm through them and takes up the box of light bulbs . . . and waits. Presently, two taps at the door.*)
SKIP	(*outside, whispers*) Right!
	(*The* PRINCE *steadies himself . . . then exits. Fade to black.*)

Scene Ten

A motorway service restaurant. Slack time of day. JO, CARL *and* SIR JAMES *approach a table,* CARL *carrying a tray of coffee and cakes. The sounds of clashing cutlery, cars zooming by on the motorway.*

JO	This one's far enough away from everyone . . .
JAMES	Sorry to drag you here . . . especially to Exit 12 . . . but I've done a good deal of confidential business in motorway cafeterias. There's an innocent anonymity about people in transit that you don't get in five-star hotels.

DIVINE RIGHT

CARL
: Where everyone thinks they've arrived and wants to know how the hell you have . . .

JAMES
: I had this sudden thought that here we are about to inaugurate the national campaign . . . and I felt that before we meet the Lib-Dems, the other parties and organisations . . . that we three needed a pre-meeting to be sure we understand one another thoroughly . . . and since we were all driving the same way, I thought it best to meet here.

JO
: I only hope my lot don't drop in on the way. (*To* CARL.) We lost four of the Labour group when they heard I'd been talking to you.

CARL
: Well I've gained six despite talking to you . . . and quite a few more who won't be named . . . some of the old Thatcherites from the eighties . . .

JO
: They don't think they can bring 'herself' back as president, do they?

CARL
: She wouldn't accept anything less than the crown.

JAMES
: My secretary counted thirty separate republican meetings in the last three weeks. It's the renunciation and the coming of the millennium. There's a mood for change. It's like a desert where it hasn't rained for years . . . yet the seeds are waiting just below the surface for the first shower of rain to bring an overnight flowering.

JO
: Overnight! I've been at this for months. It's been one long battle . . . I can show you the bruises from union meetings and working men's clubs where I've been thrown out for daring to criticise the queen. No flowering there!

CARL	You've not tasted opposition till you've had a death threat from a Conservative Women's Association. Not direct, of course. They usually call on God to do it.
JAMES	Well, we'll soon have this inaugural on top of us . . .
JO	Are the Lib-Dems in force?
JAMES	(*nods*) And the Greens and Nats . . . Charter 88 . . . and a good few late entries . . .
CARL	You should have the IEA . . .
JO	A right-wing think-tank?
CARL	They want to get rid of the Royal prerogative . . .
JO	But still want a slimmed-down monarchy.
CARL	Exactly like the IPPR . . . the left-wing think tank . . .
JAMES	Look . . . the whole purpose of me getting you both here face to face is to be absolutely sure that this inaugural is a practical ways and means meeting . . . with an all-party approach.
JO	All party except for BNP and the fascists . . . I trust you don't disagree with that?

(*She looks hard at* CARL. *He smiles.*)

CARL	They'll be there anyway . . . outside the door.
JAMES	You two will set the tone of the conference and I hope it's going to be one of avoiding party conflict.
JO	I go along with that up to a point . . . but we're by far the largest parliamentary group and we must insist on making our approach to a republic crystal clear. We want more power for parliament . . . *but* we will give powers to the president, too. We want to make a proposal today that a future president would

	take over responsibility for standards in public life . . . so that sleaze can be investigated on a permanent basis . . .
CARL	It practically *is* being investigated on a permanent basis!
JO	Only when the Prime Minister wants it investigated . . .
CARL	I thought we had a Labour Prime Minister . . .
JO	I agree that's a marginal advantage . . . but the principle remains: you can't leave corruption to the Prime Minister when the Prime Minister may be the cause of it. That's why we would want the president to take charge . . .
CARL	You don't want a president, you want a witch-finder general!
JO	Well I'm sure the right don't care a deregulator's cuss what a president may do as long as she or he does absolutely nothing!
CARL	While the left seeks to bog the presidency down in bureaucracy when it needs to be above the fray.
JO	Ah, yes! I was forgetting! There is one power you want the president to have, isn't there? I saw your article in the Spectator . . . your president would be Commander in Chief of the armed forces and have sole authority to declare war! Is that being above the fray?
CARL	You can't expect parliament to have the authority to declare war! We'd still be calling for points of order and filing into the lobbies while the missiles were in mid-air! You don't open a debate when you're about to be shot at!

(*An* ANORAKED MOTORIST *approaches with a tray, but is intimidated by the vehemence of the argument. He shuffles off.*)

JAMES	May I, like Dean Swift, make a modest proposal? That each delegation makes its statement of aims but that these are not discussed. That what we do discuss is the nature and organisation of the campaign. How we set our foot on the road from Windsor Castle . . . get from village hall to Central Hall, Westminster and the Hyde Park mass rally . . . and by what alchemy you persuade a Royal Parliament to transform itself into a republican assembly. What d'you say?

(*They both nod assent.* CARL'S *mobile bleeps.*)

CARL	Excuse me.

(*He moves away to take the call.*)

JO	I look forward to his statement. We need to know what kind of republic the right really wants.
JAMES	You may have to listen very hard.
JO	You mean not so much to hear what he has so say . . . but what he keeps avoiding saying . . .

(CARL *returns.*)

CARL	Seems our young heir apparent has gone into purdah. No press conference. No contact. No announcement. The word is that he and his advisors are not seeing eye to eye . . .
JAMES	We call ourselves a sophisticated democracy but when it comes to the issue of royal succession we all fall back helpless and leave an eighteen year old in the firing line! (*He gets to his feet.*) We'd better move.
JO	What troubles me is . . . with a new young prince before the public . . . they'll be tempted to shine up the image with half-reforms, put a lick of paint on the rotten wood and usher in Monarchy 2000.

CARL	Then that's what we've got to stop. Let's go for it Jo. Marriage of convenience.
JO	Let's call it a stand-off. Till we get what we want.
	(JAMES *invites them into a triple handshake.*)
JAMES	Thank you.
	(*They pick up their bags to go.*)
JO	Now . . . haven't had time to look at the map. Which way d'you go from Exit 15?
CARL	Haven't a clue. Jack'll tell you . . . (*She looks blank. He explains.*) My driver.
	(JO *sighs and follows. Fade to black.*)

Scene Eleven

Night. Derelict land, near West Bromwich. A mattress dumped by a rusted lorry container. The PRINCE, *disguised as before, sits, exhausted.*

He speaks into his pocket recorder.

PRINCE	Ten forty. And a moon.
	(*He can't think for a moment. Switches off and stares. Switches on.*)
	I knew it would be like stepping into someone else's world. I made a bit of a hash taking the tube from Wembley to Euston . . . changing somewhere or other. The farce was at Euston. I managed to buy a first class ticket by mistake . . . there's one window that's only first . . . I didn't realise. So I travelled second on a first class ticket. The . . . what is he . . . inspector . . . said not many people did that.
	(*He switches off, and amuses himself with the thought. He switches on.*)

Took the train to middle England . . . took a local train, then a bus . . . then walked till I came to this place. This nothing. I'd never quite realised just how broken Britain is, what a ruin we've made of it. I'm looking at, say, ten acres of derelict land . . . machine shops, factories . . . all razed to the foundations . . . a graveyard of dumped, burnt-out cars and rusted steel. This is that other kingdom we don't talk much about. To be king is not just to be king of the Sussex Downs and the Highlands . . . of Snowdonia and the Hills of Antrim . . . but also of this . . .

(*Suddenly he gets to his feet as he hears an old lady's voice from nowhere.*)

EDIE (*off*) What are you there for?

(*He takes the tape from the machine and conceals it. Snaps the machine shut, pocketing it. Again the voice.*)

(*off*) What are you there for?

PRINCE (*touch of east London*) Who's that then?

(EDIE *enters, stiff and respectable in her well-worn tweed coat.*)

EDIE What are you doing there? Well I know what. I can see what you are. You're waiting there to hurt someone . . .

PRINCE I'm not. You're alright missus. I'm not. Don' worry, alright?

EDIE What I say to them is: if you're going to kill me, kill me. I'm better there than here. All my relatives have gone and left me behind. I've got nobody now. They've all toddled off. All on a one-way ticket to the crem. Stephen's gone and Miriam. And I should have gone before Miriam. She was ten years younger than me. But there's two children gone, let alone her. And Ellen . . . and Mr Moresby who was killed at the black spot up the road. And Joyce . . .

(*She shakes her head remembering someone death shouldn't have taken.*)

Joyce! So I say: kill me. Do it . . . do it! Go on . . . kill me if you're going to. Put me in the papers.

PRINCE I'm not going to kill you . . .

EDIE I'd be better dead. There's no question. You're better dead. When you have nobody, you *are* nobody. That's what it is. Oh yes, you can kill me!

PRINCE I'll talk to you.

EDIE Why?

PRINCE I like talking.

(*She has become suspicious of him. Maybe he's insane and really will kill her.*)

EDIE Talk to yourself! It's what you were doing!

(*She exits. The* PRINCE *watches her go. He is tired out. Gets the mattress and slowly heaves it into the container. He climbs in and stretches out to sleep.* DES *and* RORKIE, *two big, shapeless, crophead young men in "combat" gear approach, quietly. They observe a moment then, at a nod from* DES, RORKIE *starts kicking the container hard. The* PRINCE *scrambles out.*)

DES Out of that, dickhead! Say your fuckin' prayers!

(*Blackout. End of Act One.*)

ACT TWO

Scene One

The same, moments later. The PRINCE *stands, wearily while* DES *walks slowly round him, inspecting, while* RORKIE, *who is in every way* DES'S *follower, grins in delight at the cat and mouse game.*

RORKIE	Maybe he don't know how to pray . . . you forgotten how to put your hands together?
DES	Maybe he's not religious . . . you religious?
	(*The* PRINCE *makes no sign.*)
RORKIE	He don't know.
DES	(*indicates container*) What were you doing in there?
	(*The* PRINCE *hesitates, tense but keeping a grip on himself.* RORKIE *uses a louder voice than* DES.)
RORKIE	Did you hear that? Are you receivin'?
PRINCE	(*east London accent*) Sleepin'.
DES	Sleeping? That's ours! That's our property!
PRINCE	Alright . . .
RORKIE	Alright? No it's not alright . . .
DES	You don't kip on someone else's property. That's what's wrong these days . . . there's no respect for property . . .
PRINCE	Didn't look like anyone's . . .
DES	Everything is someone's . . .
RORKIE	And that's ours!

DES	That's the first law of property: "Everything is someone's". Without that there'd be no law at all. You thought: heap of rusty metal. Fell off the back of a lorry . . . that's anyone's.

(*The* PRINCE *tries a lighter tone.*)

PRINCE	Okay mate . . . I'll move on then.

(RORKIE *seizes on the accent.*)

RORKIE	He's from the Smoke!
DES	Is that right? You a Londoner?

(PRINCE *nods.*)

What you doin' here then?

PRINCE	Seein' friends . . .
DES	Who?
PRINCE	People . . .
DES	What's your name?
PRINCE	Stuart.
DES	That's a Scotch name . . . Stuart. You Scotch? He's a Jock.
RORKIE	(*puzzled*) He's from London.
DES	He's a London Jock! Like there's London Paddys and London Taffs. Or Scotch Yids . . . or black as arseholes Jocks . . . fuckin mish mash! No wonder there's no room for the English!
RORKIE	Is he English?
DES	Are you English? We're English. Are you English? London English?

(*The* PRINCE *hardens his tone.*)

PRINCE	I'm British.

(Rorkie *looks threatening but* Des *motions him to keep away.*)

DES   Loyal to the Union Jack?

PRINCE   Yes.

(DES *catches the touch of irony.*)

DES   You sure.

PRINCE   (*without irony*) I'm sure.

DES   Then you're loyal to the English 'cos it's the English who rule! If you look at the Union Jack what you'll see is this big red cross in the middle . . . the cross of St George. That stands for England . . . and it's on top . . . on top of all the Jocks and Taffs and Paddys. They're where they belong . . . underneath.

(RORKIE *has been thinking.*)

RORKIE   If he's come to see his friends . . . why's he kippin' here?

PRINCE   I won't see them till tomorrow.

DES   When did you come up?

PRINCE   Today.

DES   How?

PRINCE   Train.

RORKIE   You can pay for the train . . . and you kip here?

DES   What time train?

PRINCE   Six. After the match . . .

(*He regrets saying this.*)

RORKIE   You saw England?

DES   You were there? Ticket? That'd cost yer . . .

DIVINE RIGHT

PRINCE: That's why I got no money, innit?

RORKIE: He's lying!

DES: How many penalties? How many penalties in that match?

PRINCE: Three . . .

(RORKIE *takes an evening paper out of his back pocket.*)

RORKIE: He could have read that . . .

(DES *takes the paper. On the front page is a colour photo of the cup presentation.*)

DES: You there at the presentation?

(*The* PRINCE *nods.*)

What was the Prince wearing . . . no . . . what colour tie was he wearing?

PRINCE: Tie?

DES: What colour tie?

PRINCE: This is gettin' stupid!

(*He goes to walk away but* RORKIE *stops him.*)

RORKIE: He's talking about the Prince's tie.

PRINCE: I know what he's talking about.

RORKIE: Don't say 'stupid'!

DES: What about the Prince then Stuart? Is he stupid?

(*The* PRINCE *speaks with feeling, despairing of what he's done.*)

PRINCE: Oh yes . . . oh yes . . . he really is stupid.

(RORKIE *knees him in the stomach. The* PRINCE *tries to strike him but* DES *holds his arm.*)

ACT TWO

DES No one says that about the Prince on this territory, Stuart. We are loyal to the Prince. We are loyal to the Queen. We are loyal to the Royals . . . 'cos that's what's made us what we are and all the rest our inferiors.

RORKIE England! England!

DES England is coming back my friend . . . that's the future. Shall I show you? You want to see the future?

(*From the pocket of his combat jacket he produces a cloth package. He unfolds it and shows an automatic pistol.*)

There's the future . . .

RORKIE That's what it's going to be . . .

DES Two years and we'll have more guns on the streets than the USA. Not long since we had to go to Belgium for 'em . . . now there's more for sale than the Big Issue. Why? 'Cos *they* want us to have 'em, don't they? That's why they let it be so easy.

RORKIE We train. We know how to use them.

DES The reason is the Euros. In Brussels. They want anyone to come in.

RORKIE Fuck the Euros!

DES No one's going to tell us to open our borders. No Euros . . . no yids. . .

RORKIE No Packs . . . no blacks.

BOTH 'Cos there ain't no black in the Union Jack!

DES And we'll serve Her Majesty by seeing there ain't! And as for the Republicos who want to turn out the Queen and set up an Il Presidente, like this was bongo-bongo land or fucking Brazil . . .

RORKIE	Shag 'em!
DES	We're for the Queen!

(*They burst into a hard-man version of "God Save the Queen", embellished with mock punches and kicks to a victim on the ground at their feet.*)

BOTH "God-save-our-grashus-Queen . . .

(*A grunt on the end of the line as they punch.*)

Long-live-our-noble-Queen . . .

(*A grunt as they head-butt.*)

God-save-our-Queen!

(*Three grunts on the beat as they kick the imaginary victim on the ground.* DES *will slowly point the gun at the victim through the next lines.*)

Send her victori-ass,
Happy and glori-ass,
Or get this up your arse . . .
God-save-our-Queen!

(DES *turns the gun from the victim to the* PRINCE *to do a mock shot.*)

DES	Bang!
RORKIE	Gorrim!

(*They exit. The* PRINCE *slumps slowly in anger and despair against the container wall. He checks his walkman. He stares into space. Over system we now hear the initial dialogue of the next scene as the lights fade to black.*)

Scene Two

Bedroom, CARL POINTER'S *flat. Basically a sumptuously wide bed and bedside tables with phone.*

A post-steering committee meeting for the national campaign is winding up. Jo *has been lent the bedroom phone to contact one of the Labour group.*

As she talks there should be a lot of activity around her. We hear a hubbub of voices as the members depart.

Jo   Hello. ..I'm trying to contact Philip Ross . . . yes the MP . . . This is Jo Benyon. I know he may have rung me but I'm not at my home at the moment . . . could you get him to the phone, d'you think?

(*During this* James Heaney's *secretary*, Jill, *has entered, coat on, ready to leave. She sees* Jo *on the phone and goes back to give a document to a male committee member who is putting his coat on to depart.* Jo *calls to her.*)

Jill . . . I won't be a moment . . . there's something you could do for me if you would . . .

(Jill *returns, opens her case and checks through it while waiting.* Jo *is back on phone.*)

Yes . . . Philip! At last! We've just finished a National Campaign meeting and I haven't been able to get to the phone. Yes, we're using Carl Pointer's flat . . . alright? Have you heard about Wednesday? Yes, there's an emergency debate called . . . I know! I'll read you the motion.

(Jill *hands her a piece of paper.*)

"That this House is concerned about the present situation of the monarchy and wishes to re-affirm its support for the Crown." No . . . "its total support for the Crown." What? Yes it's a Tory leadership motion . . . hold on would you?

(CARL *and a* CHAUFFEUR *have entered and* JO *stops and puts her hand over the receiver.* CARL, *apologising on the move, goes to his bedside table and extracts a bunch of keys.*)

CARL Two shakes!

(*He returns, tossing the keys to the* CHAUFFEUR.)

I'm not here . . .

(*He and the* CHAUFFEUR *exit.* JO *resumes on phone.*)

JO Sorry . . . minor interruption . . . the point is that the Tories want to appease their backbenchers who think that their leadership and ours are doing an undercover deal on reforming the monarchy . . . which they are, but in doing so they've given us exactly what we've been wanting . . . a platform for republicanism . . . and it all coincides beautifully with our national rally at Central Hall this weekend! Listen . . . I'm meeting the others at half past midnight at my flat . . . could you? Wonderful! Will you do your thing on the costs of the monarchy? Good. Going to fax you now . . . See you later.

(*Puts phone down.* JAMES *has entered during this and whispered something into* JILL'S *ear.* JILL *is about to go.*)

JAMES (*to* JO) I'm sorry. You finished?

JO Yes. Here's the fax number, Jill. Attention of Philip Ross . . . thanks a lot.

(*She hands over a couple of A4 sheets.* JILL *nods and exits quickly.*)

That was the last of the Labour group. They're all informed now . . . we'll be meeting later. I still can't believe it! We've got the debate!

You duck and weave and struggle then it all falls into your lap!

(CARL *has entered with a tray of coffee and sandwiches. He puts it on the bedside table.*)

CARL
Some of these left over.

(*Phone rings.* Jo *takes it. Listens briefly as she is told the cost of her calls.*)

JO
(*to operator*) Thanks.

(*Puts phone down and takes money from her bag.*)

CARL
That meeting was a disaster area. A dozen people coming to two dozen wrong conclusions!

JAMES
We have the rally well organised for Central Hall. That done, I was happy to let them have their say.

(JO *hands money to* CARL.)

JO
For my calls. James you witness. We are not being subsidised by the right. And thanks for the use of your bedroom.

CARL
My pleasure . . . (*Carrying on his exchange with* JAMES.) Look, there was too much time wasting . . . The Welsh Nationalists! Give us a break! I don't mind a bit of historical background but I draw the line at the eleventh century.

JAMES
Well, you see . . . I thought the nationalists very solid. Very strong for the campaign. The Scot-Nats have been fielding republicans and getting them elected for years. You have to see it as creative conflict . . . opposites coming together, striking sparks off each other and producing ideas. Like you and Jo. What we need now is the energy flowing. We can move to consensus later.

CARL	Consensus? I don't want consensus. I want some shape and thrust to the movement!
JO	You only believe in a consensus of one, don't you Carl?
CARL	The other kind don't work . . .
JO	But everything's changed now. The heir to the throne abdicates and the next locks himself away in the Palace, or wherever, and we have the debate!
CARL	And I get crucified. It's too soon. All tomorrow's going to show is how little backing I have.
JO	It's the foot in the door . . .
CARL	Yes, well I'd feel happier if there was a body attached to it!
JAMES	You notice everyone had heard the same rumour that the prince has asked for a referendum.
JO	It's like asking the whole nation for an oath of loyalty . . .
CARL	They'll talk him out of it.
JO	So they should. He can't have a referendum. He might win it!
CARL	In which case he'd lose. Because then the monarchy would depend on the will of the people.
JO	Instead of being ordained by God.
JAMES	All the same, the government may hold a referendum. Not on the monarchy . . . but on those piecemeal reforms you're afraid of . . . reducing the size and cost . . . and cutting the connection with the Church of England.

Jo	The church! Well, they'll win that one. There are less church-goers these days than there are Lib-Dems. But if they want any kind of reform they'll have to set up a committee and what we have to do on Wednesday is leave no one in any doubt that it must allow room to discuss the republican alternative!
JAMES	Well, if both of you are on the committee . . .
CARL	They'll never choose me. She'll be on.
Jo	You think?
CARL	The PM has to put you on it. He can't be seen to be censoring your views. You may get up his nose but he daren't make you a martyr.
JAMES	With that hope before us I'll say good night. We're all going to be working late.
CARL	Not me. Mine's a breakfast meeting.
JAMES	(*to* Jo) I look forward to hearing you.
Jo	I hate these speaking Olympics . . . especially since the government has a way of awarding itself the prizes before the race has begun. But I'm glad it's here.
JAMES	God bless.
Jo	Good night.

(*He bends to kiss her and exits,* CARL *going with him to see him out.*)

CARL	(*off*) I still think we should sharpen the focus, James.
JAMES	(*off*) Well . . . Wednesday should tell us a lot. Good night.
CARL	(*off*) Good night.

(While she's left alone, Jo sits back on the bed to make a few notes . . . then, feeling the comfort of the bed, slips off her shoes and puts her feet up. CARL returns and surveys her a moment.)

JO Just a thought or two . . .

CARL It could be policy tomorrow to carry on as we have in the campaign . . . to argue for the end of the monarchy . . . and the broad principles of a republic. Getting into detail could weaken the case.

JO You seemed to be saying the opposite just now. I know what you've been doing Carl. You've been biding your time to start nudging the campaign in your direction because you feel you can make a far better showing on public platforms than you can in the House. So now it *has* come to the House you'd like the Labour Group to stick to generalities . . . in case our idea of a republic begins to become the accepted one.

CARL Right! I don't see a future president as a referee, as you do . . . but as a key player.

JO Ah! Are we going to hear about this then?

(CARL sighs, pommels his head, then walks over, kicks off his shoes and joins her on the bed.)

CARL It's not so easy to argue the case thoroughly because it means arguing against my own party and the business community that gave me all my breaks. You see, the problem with British business people is that success softens them . . . where it should sharpen. And d'you know why this is? The Country House Factor. They get to three hundred thousand a year . . . with share options taking them past their second million . . . and all of a sudden their minds turn to the Country House . . . the

>   Queen Anne residence with lake and lawns
>   and landscaped rolling acres in good fox
>   hunting country . . . they may have despised
>   it. They may have thought it no longer existed.
>   But as long as the monarchy exists, it will
>   exist . . . because at the centre of the Country
>   House Culture, promoting it, sustaining it, are
>   the Royals. It's their way of life. They have
>   this infinite capacity for re-inventing the
>   nineteenth century. And doesn't it look
>   seductive to your battle-weary entrepreneur
>   sitting in a smoke glass block in the City!
>   Instead of the dawn raids and hostile
>   takeovers and eternal jetting from one bush
>   fire to another, you exchange it all for a
>   permanent role in a never-ending Merchant
>   Ivory movie.

JO   Why didn't it happen to you?

CARL   It almost did. I'd earmarked the house . . .
            married a woman who rode to hounds . . .

JO   Your wife kills foxes?

CARL   Oh yes . . .

JO   How disgusting!

CARL   Ah, you mustn't think of it as a fox . . . not
            smart, debonair, dashing Mr Fox. She'll tell
            you . . . a fox is vermin. Think of it as a rat . . .

JO   They'd look pretty silly chasing a rat!

CARL   They do in any case. I remember my father
            having to kow-tow to them. All the
            countryside means to me is poverty and
            humiliation. Those people were my enemy.

JO   Why aren't you a socialist?

CARL   Because I'm against suicide. Socialism is
            collectivism and collectivism is the process of
            wanting everyone to get in the lifeboat despite
            the fact that if you get everybody in . . . it
            sinks.

(Jo *closes her eyes wearily.*)

This bed vibrates, if you want it to . . .

Jo It what?

Carl It vibrates, electronically. There's a white button on the console on your side. Try it . . .

Jo Why?

Carl Tones up the body. Takes your tiredness away.

(*She presses a button. An electronic hum. She feels the high-frequency vibrations.*)

Well?

(*She turns it off.*)

Jo It's obscene . . . Like being harassed by a mattress!

(*She gets off the bed feeling this might be taken as a cue of some kind.*)

It's obscene the money people like you make . . . and it's obscene the toys you spend it on. I want a wash.

Carl Use the power shower. Ten high pressure jets that hit you from different angles. A ritual cleansing combined with a primal massage.

Jo Even your plumbing has fascist tendencies. Don't you have a simple wash basin?

(*He indicates the bathroom.*)

Thanks.

(*She exits to the bathroom. We hear her splashing her face.*)

Carl My dilemma is that I thought I was joining a party of leadership . . . whereas what I now find is a party in full retreat. The future's with Europe . . . but they run away from it because they've drawn the conclusion they can never lead it. If we can't lead, we won't play. So we turn inwards to warm beer and village greens and start re-hashing the cold leavings of a country that never really was . . . not so much Little Englander as Garden Gnome Englander . . .

(Jo *has returned, towelling her face.*)

But I believe we *can* lead Europe . . . it's not a question of economic strength but of attitude. I don't think the Germans want to and I don't think the French can. The Germans are too afraid of what happened last time they tried to lead Europe and the French are too happy being beneficiaries. There's a vacuum there to be filled. We can fill it . . . but we must make ourselves want to. What the republic must do is make us want power.

(Jo *shakes her head.*)

Jo	What the republic must do is make us want justice.
Carl	You're a politician . . . you want power!
Jo	Yes . . . but only as a means of achieving justice.
Carl	Then you don't want it. Or won't admit it. Justice is of the head. Power is a more basic urge . . .

(*He comes close to her.*)

You have to want it like you want sex.

Jo	Oh, if it's like sex . . . sometimes you want it and sometimes you don't. Like now. I don't. But there you are, we'll both be having it tomorrow. Wasn't it Edwina who said that a speech in the House is better than an orgasm?

And in the House you can have it in front of six hundred people . . .

(*She moves away and gets her things together.*)

CARL Never been a case of rape between honourable members, has there?

JO No. Surprising really . . . because, if the House dealt with it, the rapist would get off with a slap on the wrist from the Speaker and a mild reprimand from the Committee of Privileges.

(*He picks up the tray and offers.*)

CARL Okay doll. Take some sandwiches instead.

JO Good idea.

(*She folds one in a napkin and puts it in her case.*)

I think this bed that you and I are supposed to have got into . . . it's time we got well and truly out of it.

(*The door buzzer is heard.*)

Who's this? Some of your friends?

(*She exits to bathroom.*)

CARL Probably the resident hooker doing her rounds.

(*He exits to front door. We hear* JAMES *returning.*)

JAMES (*off*) I'm sorry Carl. May I clean up?

(JO, *hearing this, re-enters.*)

JO James?

(CARL *and the* CHAUFFEUR *lead in* JAMES, *who has mud stains on his coat and holds his handkerchief to a cut on his face. On seeing* JO, JAMES *explains.*)

JAMES
I tried a debate with a BNP group outside Green Park Station . . . but I found their arguments a bit too convincing.

JO
You've been hit!

JAMES
Once with a Union Jack . . . then with something small, hard and jagged . . . though probably not one of the crown jewels.

(JO *has run to the bathroom and returned with a wet cloth. She bathes* JAMES'S *hand. Meanwhile* CARL *has murmured an instruction to the* CHAUFFEUR, *who exits to living room.*)

CARL
He'll ring my GP.

JAMES
No . . .

CARL
Yes . . .

(CARL *goes to the bathroom and returns with water and a first aid box.* JO *uses a tissue to clean the cut.*)

JO
What were they doing?

JAMES
Spray painting our posters. Looking for trouble.

JO
(*to* CARL) These are your people!

CARL
Don't be stupid!

JO
I asked you to condemn them, clearly and publicly, and you wouldn't!

CARL
I condemn all violence.

JO
Them! I'm talking about them! The right!

CARL
I haven't heard you criticising the Trots!

(JAMES *feels rather neglected.*)

JAMES: It's come to something when the wounded arrive at the first aid post and the medics are too busy fighting each other!

CARL: I'll see if he's got through.

(*He exits to sitting room.*)

JAMES: I'll draw up a condemnation of the right wing violence for all to sign. He can't refuse.

JO: The one qualm I've always had about this is that, somehow, the monarchy draws the sting of the right and in a republic they'll be harder to control.

JAMES: At the beginning of World War II there were members of the royal family ready to side with Hitler. No, I'd say, without them, the right will have less to focus on.

JO: With your optimism you should be in the House.

JAMES: I think you mean that with my optimism I should stay well out of it!

(*Fade to black.*)

Scene Three

Noon. Bright garish day in an unvisited corner of a tacky new-ish but already deteriorating shopping mall. A post-modernist bench and saplings in concrete tubs.

The PRINCE, *now maybe in sunglasses, sits and comments into his recorder.*

PRINCE: Noon. I'm in what calls itself a town centre. But I daren't ask which town. It's some great plaything of a place, rising out of the crumbling streets. A children's toy for shopping in . . . where brick is beautiful but the pretty post-modernist alloy railings have razor-headed spikes. You feel you are not so much on earth as in one of those replicas of earth conjured up in Sci-Fi movies by the insane emperor of Alpha Centauri. In the innocent doorway of the Ethnic Artifacts Boutique a silver man is waiting to zap one. I've found a vacant corner . . . thirty yards from where the shoppers flow past like a river . . . above me the giant duct that puffs out stale air and the smells of chocolate waffles and mozzarella cheese . . .

I suppose it's been proved by research that these dreamlands predispose people to buy. But where they consume . . . who cares?

(*He is joined by* GREG. *Thirty-ish. Very expensive casuals. He sits and drinks in the sun . . . noting the way the* PRINCE *tries to put away the recorder without drawing attention to it.*)

GREG   You got his tape?

PRINCE Tape?

(GREG *indicates the recorder.*)

GREG   Playing his tape . . .

PRINCE Who's tape?

GREG   You don't know?

PRINCE No.

GREG   No?

PRINCE I was just checking it . . .

(*He means the recorder. He pockets it.*)

GREG   He won't let you record him. You buy his tape or CD. You not been in the mall before?

PRINCE	No.
GREG	So you really don't know who I'm talking about?
PRINCE	Honest.
GREG	Never mind. He'll be here . . . you'll know then.

GREG: (*He goes back to basking in the sun but soon a shadow drifts across.*)

I sit down . . . a cloud comes over the sun. You know what the first boss I ever worked for told me?

(*He has an insistent way of requiring an answer.*)

PRINCE	No . . . what?
GREG	"The sun is always there". Eh? Eh?

(*The PRINCE humours him.*)

PRINCE	Yeah . . .
GREG	"The sun is always there!"

(*The cloud passes and the sun shines again.*)

You see! He said "You may think it's gone . . . it's left you. But it's still there! Behind the clouds or at night time on the other side of the earth . . . still there. It's only hidden. And where it is . . . thought we can't see it, it's as bright and untarnished brilliant as it always is! The sun is never grey." Was he right?

PRINCE	Right.
GREG	Every businessman starting out to hustle should have that over his desk. You may feel grey. The sun isn't. And it's always there . . .
PRINCE	Yeah . . .

GREG   I flew in from Malaga yesterday. No spot on earth like Malaga. Been living down there five years now. Really ace! There's only one word for it and that's "ambience". It is ambient. Everything about it is ambient. (*Thinks about this.*) And the talent! (*Does a nudge-nudge expression.*) First day I got there to look at some villa they were shooting a movie along the coast . . . a whole squadron of Moroccan cavalry with turbans and lances and pennants fluttering. Horse's heads tossing . . . all drawn up along by the deep blue sea. Some 'Casablanca' type movie.

PRINCE   Straight up?

GREG   No really. And all the British ex-pats down there had come out of their villas to watch. Every villain and law-breaker you could imagine! Chestfulls of grey hair. Accents like yours. Bimbo on each tattooed arm. I thought: this is where they got to! These are the Brits who got away. Did it . . . got it and left. These are the Brits who come up from below . . . from the streets. No education . . . which is the secret. If you get educated all that happens is you end up working for those with money . . . instead of having money. The trick in life is to go from where there's no money . . . round the educated classes to where those with the money are . . . and lift some of it off them. Like, in a way, I did. (*He hastens to correct any wrong impression.*) I mean I had to work for it . . . *but* . . . I mean *but*. I drop out of school straight into a sleepy little family estate agents. Didn't take me long to realise what the concept should be. What the boss thought he was doing was selling houses. What I realised was that you should be selling them the *idea* of moving. It's in the mind! It's aspirations! And I could sell that. You got a home?

PRINCE   Not of my own . . .

GREG	Still at mum and dad's?
	(*The* PRINCE *nods, warily.*)
	So what I would be selling you is the aspiration of the young independent spirit . . . not just a home, right?
PRINCE	Right.
GREG	So I revamp the agency. Re-write the ads. I create a new image and the boss makes me a partner at twenty one! It's the housing boom. We make money! Then along comes one of the biggest national building societies, now turned into a bank, the Town and Country . . . and buys us . . . as part of a chain. With that and a property deal I, son of a hardware salesman, am a millionaire at twenty five. You like that story?
PRINCE	It's a good story . . . yes.
GREG	And the joke is that after they bought us came the crash. Plus they didn't know how to run a local agency. They bought the good will . . . but the good will was us. The good will was me. And they let me get away to Malaga. Become an ex-pat . . . I just come back now and then to see my mum . . . she won't move, I can't persuade her. I tell her the solemn truth, as I tell you . . . the only happy Brits today are ex-pat Brits . . . I mean at your and my level. Not chairmen of gas or water . . . Ex-pats. What d'you do?
PRINCE	Unemployed . . .
GREG	You see! What's your line?
PRINCE	Jus' left school, ain't I?
GREG	Look. Quit. Cross the channel and backpack down to Malaga.
	(*He hands him a card.*)

	Buzz my buzzer and I guarantee you'll have a week's bed and meals till you're on your feet. You'll love it. We laugh a lot. They say money doesn't bring happiness . . . they're lying. We jump in the Med and we laugh and laugh . . . we laugh through the food and the wine and the sex . . . and the sun is always there! Right?
Prince	Right.
Greg	Money follows the sun, my friend. California, Florida, Malaga, Monte . . . that's where it all ends up . . . so when you're there you sense it near you, ready to be reached for . . . yeh?
Prince	Yeah.
Greg	Like the fruit you hold precious in your hand . . .

(*The* Prince *is less certain what this means.*)

Prince	Right.
Greg	Just buzz me. Okay? There's nothing we've got here that isn't better down there. Better golf courses, better weather, better sea that's ever-warm and better views of blue mountains, ever-capped with snow. Better bullfights, better flamenco . . . better royals.

(*The* Prince *looks questioningly.*)

King Juan Carlos of Spain! He has dignity . . . he's clever and he doesn't cost a lot. Whereas ours! They're about as dignified as the News of the World but only half as intelligent. Bunch of tarts and snobs! And they cost an arm and a leg. You see, Juan Carlos has the talent for it. He belongs on red carpet . . . just as they belong on bananna skins.

(ROCKY, *and old country singer who frequents this pitch arrives with one-man band set-up of foot drum, cymbal, guitar and harmonica. Maybe he is assisted by a beer gut companion to set up. The country singer is in old jeans suit and wears blue specs and stetson.*)

Scene Four

Westminster. The LEADER OF THE OPPOSITION *is on his feet.*

L OPP ... Within half a mile of this house, Madam Speaker ... petrol bombs ... offensive weapons ... mayhem on the streets because this so-called British Republican Movement is intent on using violence to get its way ...

(*He gives way to the* PM.)

PM The right honourable gentleman exaggerates, Madam Speaker. The police noted one petrol device ... and I deplore it ... as I deplore all violence ... as I ... and I hope I take him with me in this ... as I deplore those who call themselves royalists and attack legitimate political meetings and demonstrations.

L OPP Madam Speaker ... I repudiate any on this side of the house who seek to stir up trouble. But now ... will the Prime Minister repudiate that caucus of Republicans in his party who make it their business to inflame the situation?

PM I have condemned all violence, Madam Speaker, and do so again now!

L OPP But not those who hide behind you and provoke it!

PM I repeat ... *all* violence!

L OPP That's evading the question!

(*Through this, fade to black.*)

Scene Five

A street. Somewhere in the Midlands. A silent rank of police in riot gear. Visors up. Distant sounds of fire engine sirens and a march with organised opposition. A POLICE OFFICER *quietly addresses his squad.*

OFFICER Hold yourselves steady . . . stay relaxed. This is not Apocalypse Now. It is not even Apocalypse in the next two minutes. This is a situation which, by using our professional nous and experience we can easily de-escalate and render unharmful. It says in the book. There are certain eastern mystics . . . holy men . . . who, they tell us, can actually lower their blood pressure by the power of the mind. It's been measured on instruments. So at times of stress they can calm themselves. Now that's a course we should all have been sent on. Better than "Modern Management and Marketing Skills in Relation to Law Enforcement" . . . especially at this moment in time. What you see before you is the malaise of the British nation . . . which is like a captainless team that has lost its umpires and can't find the rules. On one side we have a second coming of skins, the Front. BNP, Column 18, etc . . . the new Doc Marten monarchists. On the other side, a loose Anti Nazi association of left wing splinter groups, some of which are hoping to hijack the republican bus and drive it to a depot called "Dictatorship". We, of course, are piggy in the middle, representing the vast, silent, law-abiding majority . . . and thinking why the blank fucking blank aren't they out here with us?

(*Sounds of the march suddenly increase as marchers round a corner ahead. The police lower their visors.*)

Right! Remember your training. Sabre rattling commence!

(*The line of police parts to allow the* Officer *to take his position in the rear. Officers begin to bang batons against riot shields. Fade to black.*)

Scene Six

A twenty four hour shop in the Midlands. Just before dawn. There's something of everything in the 7-11 manner. Coffee and tea machine. Groceries. Confectionary. Newspapers. The Night Manager, *a Nigerian in a smart uniform, is stacking the morning papers on the display unit.* Rena, *a bag lady, is singing to him in a low, mocking tone. "When a man loves a woman . . ." In a corner, a* Middle-aged Man *in 'smart casuals', but looking tense and worn out, drinks a cup of coffee and pretends to inspect the shelves.*

As the Manager *opens the bundles of papers he pauses to skin through a tabloid. The headline reads: PRINCE GOES MISSING.*

Rena	(*to* Manager) You looked at me. You did . . . you looked. I saw it. Little sidelong look. Ping! Eyes creeping over for a little look. They all try not to look. They all keep them fixed forward like this! Then brrrring! They have to look.
Manager	Alright . . .
Rena	I'm here! You have to notice me . . .
Manager	I have noticed.
Rena	I'm here!
Manager	You'll get nothing else . . .
Rena	I'm here!
Manager	I bloody know you're there by the shocking niff . . .

RENA	Have I embarrassed you?
MANAGER	It's time to go, Rena.
RENA	No . . . it's really cold . . .
MANAGER	People comin' in time.
RENA	Wait till the sun comes up.
MANAGER	No.

(*The PRINCE enters and hangs back uneasily, trying to get the hang of the place.*)

RENA	Till the sun comes up . . .
MANAGER	No.
RENA	Till there's some sun.
MANAGER	What you talking about, Rena? You can't stay till the sun comes up because when the light strikes you have to go back to the churchyard and climb in your coffin.

(*He enjoys the thought as he goes about his work. RENA is genuinely put down and hurt. The PRINCE, obviously cold, approaches the MANAGER.*)

PRINCE	Gorra tea, mate?
MANAGER	In the machine man. 60p.

(*The PRINCE finds the money. Goes to the machine. Takes a careful look at how it works. RENA crosses to him.*)

RENA	Mornin' . . .
MANAGER	Hey . . . no beggin'.

(*He indicates that she should be off. The PRINCE puts his hand in his pocket. The MANAGER shakes his head.*)

Don't give. Not on the premises.

(*The* PRINCE *complies.*)

RENA Then I'll have to find the Prince.

(*The* PRINCE *turns, sharply. His eye falls on a newspaper.*)

I shall look for him in the night. I shall find him beneath the stars. He's bound to give to me since we're both on the road. He can be Prince of Wanderers now. King of cardboard city. I talk a lot of crap. I was a stewardess on a cruise ship once. You had to talk a lot of crap. He'll give me a couple of quid. He's soft enough. D'you see him with his bags and papers under the motorway?

(*She goes to exit, then watches as the* PRINCE *fiddles with the tea machine. She offers instructions.*)

Press his little button. Good night and morning. Good morning, good night. (*Pause.*) Good mornight . . .

(*She looks hopefully at the* MANAGER *but he looks stonily ahead. She exits. The* PRINCE *gets the tabloid. He looks vaguely for the price, finds it and pays.*)

MANAGER Cold?

PRINCE Yeah.

MANAGER It's cold.

(*The* PRINCE *moves away to read the paper and drink his tea. Presently the middle-aged man,* MARK, *moves to him and speaks confidentially.*)

MARK I hope you don't mind me asking but have you been to one of the clubs?

PRINCE	Clubs?
MARK	Clubbing. Disco-ing.
PRINCE	I know what you mean. No . . .
MARK	Looking for my daughter. She's out . . . clubbing. They could be still at it till now. I don't know. Could they, d'you think?
PRINCE	Well . . .
MARK	You don't know.
PRINCE	No.
MARK	I see a bit of this place. Looking for her.

(*Indicates the headline in the paper.*)

Ironic . . . they're looking for their son. I'm divorced. It's partly what does it isn't it? I say that, because I don't know. I begged her not to leave me . . . and she hasn't entirely. She comes back from time to time. I have a son as well as a daughter. He's alright. It all seems to have hit her. He's reading law. She spends most of her time breaking it. So . . . I go to bed. Can't sleep. Get up . . . go round the clubs. You ask the bouncers, "Is Janie Hargreaves in there?" They won't tell you. I'll go mad with it. She's tearing herself apart. Thin as a shadow. (*Indicates paper again.*) In a way they're to blame. |
| PRINCE | Who? |
| MARK | The royal family. I suppose you can't expect them all to have held together when everything else was falling apart, can you? You just hoped they'd be the exception and they weren't. It's all gone. All slithered away. All the props, one by one . . . marriage, the church, the royal family . . . even Parliament. They used to resign once . . . MPs . . . Ministers, caught up in the least thing, they'd resign. Resign over sixpence! Over some ill- |

judged remark. They resigned over their own accord. Didn't wait to be sacked. There was an inward voice then that told us. Not now. Now it's a downward slope, an inclined plane, tipping over into everything goes. Sleeping together . . . living together, bonking, bum boys, one parent families . . . anorexia . . . anabolic steroids . . . crack . . . HIV. Why couldn't the royal family have held the line? I reckon that would have stemmed things just enough to turn the corner and recover somehow. (*Pause.*) Janie's going to kill herself. (*Points to paper.*) And if that young man can't make the commitment for life . . . for life! Well, that's what it is . . . for life. Actually keeping vows . . . you know, actually keeping them . . . then he might as well drop out like everybody else does and we can all go on spiralling out of control without him.

PRINCE   Why put it all on him? Why load it all on his back? If everything's in free fall . . . if it's all flown apart then its on millions of consciences to make a stand about it — not just him. But you don't need him at all. Why d'you need him? Get a goat. Get a four legged, bleating goat. Take it up to a high cliff edge. Load all the nation's troubles on it, slit its gullet and fling it over! It's you. All of you. Not him!

MARK   I had no right to go on like that. I thought you were just another "clubber". Time to take myself off home. I'm too depressing. I'm sorry to bend your ear . . .

PRINCE   (*back in accent*) No, s'okay. Not to worry. S'okay. You got more than your share.

MARK   It's her, you see. I can still see her as a child. On the beach. Looking at me. Asking me . . . asking me! "Can I go in the sea, daddy?"

(*He exits. The* MANAGER *has heard most of it.*)

MANAGER   Who is that?

PRINCE   He's looking for his daughter.

MANAGER   He should think what he says about the royal
                    family. I come from Nigeria. We have a
                    situation there that should make everyone here
                    hang on to what they've got. Our head of state
                    is the army. Our government is the army. You
                    want a magistrate? The army. Do a business
                    deal . . . the army. Let him live in a
                    dictatorship and that would teach him the
                    value of the queen. (*He has brought out an
                    electric polisher.*) Like a job? Polish the
                    floor? Only take twenty minutes and I'll pay
                    you a hamburger or a cheeseburger and jumbo
                    coffee.

                    (*The PRINCE looks at the floor.*)

PRINCE   Polish it? What do you do?

                    (*The MANAGER demonstrates the polisher.*)

MANAGER   Turn him on . . . turn him off. Nice slow
                    circles all the way round. A deal?

PRINCE   A deal.

                    (*The PRINCE switches on and starts to polish.
                    Fade to black.*)

Scene Seven

*Parliament. Debate in progress. Roars of derision and
approval.* PM *rises.*

PM   Madam Speaker . . . I'll repeat what I said . . .
                    though I thought it was perfectly clear. The
                    Prince has decided to take a few days away
                    from his normal duties to consider what the
                    whole of this House wishes to consider,
                    namely those changes, those reforms
                    appropriate to the monarchy in this day and
                    age . . .

(GIERSON *rises*.)

GIERSON — But where is he, Madam Speaker? Where's he gone? Can the Prime Minister let us in on it?

PM — I thought my honourable friend would be the last to be peddling tabloid speculation in this House . . .

GIERSON — Do you know?

PM — No, Madam Speaker, I don't know . . . and I respect the decision of the Palace not to tell us since the whole object of his temporary absence is to remain undisturbed and escape the attentions of the press.

(*The* SPEAKER *nods to the* LEADER OF THE OPPOSITION, *who now stands*.)

L OPP — Well, Madam Speaker, this is very strange. The mood music we keep on getting from the Prime Minister is that of concern for the prince and . . . give and take some unspecified reforms . . . support for the monarchy. So why are we still waiting for him to denounce those in his own ranks who seek to destroy the monarchy . . . as I denounce them on this side of the House?

(*The* PM *comes to the box*.)

PM — Madam Speaker, I do wish the leader of the party opposite would share my view that a debate is a place for argument, not denunciation.

CARL — As one of those denounced, Madam Speaker, I would object to the accusation that I seek to destroy the monarchy. Why should I when the monarchy has shown itself perfectly capable of carrying out its own destruction without any help from me!

SPEAKER — I will remind the House that it is an abiding tradition that honourable members do not criticise the monarch or individual members of the royal family.

CARL
I singled no one out, Madam Speaker . . .

SPEAKER
You came close to it.

(*She nods to the* LEADER OF THE OPPOSITION *who has risen as* CARL *sits*.)

L OPP
Could I hold the Prime Minister to the point, Madam Speaker? If he says we must debate with these republicans then let him answer their arguments. We are talking of a fringe tendency, Madam Speaker. An earnest group of eccentrics who want a grey and boring Britain instead of a colourful, Royal Britain. They would want us to visit Republican Ascot and the Republican Opera House . . . go to the Republican National Theatre or the Republican Shakespeare Company!

(GIERSON *intervenes*.)

GIERSON
Well, they could still keep the same logo!

L OPP
I have news for the honourable gentleman. What they and the vast majority of this nation really wish to keep is the monarchy. Let me simply tackle one of the republican central arguments: they criticise the monarchy for being based on the principle of heredity . . . inheritance. They say this is not democratic or meritocratic . . . (*He turns and glances at* CARL.) Yet all of us base our family lives on that very principle of inheritance. Every time loving parents leave the family home to be divided among their children, they are operating this same principle of heredity. Elderly people who forego some pleasure for themselves so that money can be passed on to their grandchildren are acting on this very principle. Heredity . . . it is a symbol of care and continuance . . . a Christian symbol of love . . . not of self, but of those we bring into

	this world. It is deeply spiritual. It will never change because its presence in us comes directly from God.
SPEAKER	Jo Benyon . . .
JO	(*rising to speak*) Finally he touched on it, Madam Speaker! Not so much an argument . . . more a refuge . . . the ultimate refuge of all royalists . . . the last resort of all monarchists . . . God and Divine Right. Divine Right . . . the concept we none of us believe in . . . yet we carry on behaving as though we did. That God has given the monarch the right to rule. I mean no disrespect to God . . . (*Sceptical reactions.*) No . . . no. There are many believing republicans! We are drawn from all persuasions . . . but the problem is that, if you ask the bishops of the church these days, you will find very little certainty even amongst them as to what god is! From the Old Testament authoritarian God to a collection of fluid moral concepts . . . no one agrees any more. And if they can't agree on how we relate to God, how can anyone agree on God's relationship to the throne? But if Divine Right isn't valid, by what right does the monarch rule? some would say tradition . . . custom. Be careful! Customs come and go. It was the custom, apparently, until twenty five years ago for the National Anthem to be played in cinemas and theatres before or after every single performance while the audience stood to attention! Suddenly that custom disappeared. Custom is a fragile thread for so weighty a matter as the right to rule! But then, the majority of this House might well say the monarch has the right to rule by public acclaim. And if I ask what acclaim, they would say the opinion polls, though they would say it shamefacedly, as people who totally discount opinion polls always do. Of course, all republicans would like to see a Head of State by public acclaim . . . in a

proper election with a choice of candidates. The trouble with monarchy is that, with no choice, once the acclaim dwindles, you have a minority monarch. Does this House, Madam Speaker, wish to condemn the monarchy to a lingering death . . . or does it rather wish to take the courageous decision now . . . and say to the present descendants of the monarchy, "Thank you for the past thousand years. The next thousand lie in a new direction . . ."

(*Fade to black.*)

Scene Eight

LYDIA WEST'S *flat in Wolverhampton.*

The radio plays bluesy music. LYDIA *is face to face with the* PRINCE, *still dressed as before. It is a moment or two after she has let him into her living room. A stack of the days papers on the floor.*

LYDIA	It's you!
PRINCE	(*no assumed accent*) I had planned to phone you first, but I felt someone might recognise me between the call box and here and then I might have thought it better not to arrive . . .
LYDIA	I wasn't going to let you in. Well, I wouldn't let someone like you in, would I?
PRINCE	I've been out there from 8:00 AM. Thought I'd catch you as you got on your way to school. Then when you did come out you'd got the little girl with you . . .
LYDIA	My daughter.
PRINCE	Daughter?
LYDIA	Cathy. I've just taken her to playgroup.
PRINCE	Well, that's it, you see . . . I almost gave up. I thought you'd gone to work.

(*He sways slightly.*)

LYDIA You okay?

PRINCE Bit bushed . . .

(*She indicates a seat. He sits.*)

LYDIA I mean . . . should I be calling you 'sir'?

(*He just smiles.*)

PRINCE I'm like a walking bomb. I thought I mustn't endanger you with . . . Cathy?

(*She nods.*)

I keep thinking the press may be round the next corner. Didn't want you all over the papers as well as me . . .

LYDIA You are all over the papers, aren't you?

PRINCE You seem to have a good selection.

(*He indicates a stack of newspapers.*)

LYDIA Well I have an interest, don't I? I met you. I'm sorry, you'll have to do without the "sir".

(*Her antagonism towards him returns momentarily.*)

PRINCE I think someone who's presented himself to people as something he isn't doesn't deserve a lot of respect.

LYDIA What have you been doing?

PRINCE Bummed around. Slept rough. One has had rather an uncomfortable time.

(*His tone is self-mocking.*)

LYDIA Why? Why do that?

PRINCE To talk to people without them knowing who I was.

LYDIA	But they'd know when you spoke.
PRINCE	I used my all-purpose EastEnders . . . (*Drops into accent.*) "Ahs it goin' missus? Gorra tea mate?"
LYDIA	This is ridiculous!

(*But he is suddenly serious.*)

PRINCE	No.
LYDIA	You want some tea?
PRINCE	I thought I could pretend to have nothing . . . so I could talk to people who had nothing. Shouldn't you be going to school?
LYDIA	Not this morning as it happens. Not till break. My class is in choir practice. I'll just phone in, d'you mind? (*Taps out number on phone. Into phone.*) Jean there . . . ? Could you? I'll hang on. (*As she listens she smiles.*) I can hear them singing in the hall. "Jerusalem".

(*She presses the 'loud' button and we hear the children singing "Jerusalem" faintly in the background. The* PRINCE *smiles as he listens. Then* JEAN *comes on.*)

JEAN	(*on phone*) You Liddy?
LYDIA	I don't think you'll need to but could you cover if I'm not in till break?
JEAN	(*on phone*) Anytime . . . you okay?
LYDIA	Yeah . . . something's come up. See you. (*She puts phone down.*) You know the line, "Till we have built Jerusalem in England's green and pleasant land"?

(*The* PRINCE *nods.*)

I could never get them to understand it . . . well what it meant to me . . . it was "the green

	and pleasant land" that puzzled them. I mean . . . where's that round here? (*She looks at him carefully.*) You have slept rough, haven't you?
PRINCE	I got paranoia about hotels. Thought I'd be seen through.
LYDIA	You've got bits all over you . . . (*She removes one from his jacket.*) Now this isn't a dream. You don't touch things like this in dreams.
PRINCE	No. It's not a dream because we're talking. You notice you don't get much talk in dreams. Apparently it's because we need to keep the hearing facility going while we're asleep . . . for emergencies.
LYDIA	Why this area?
PRINCE	It's where I chose to come to.
	(*She suspects he might have come to see her deliberately, which, of course, is true.*)
LYDIA	Oh yes . . . you had my address.
PRINCE	I had my secretary take the addresses of everyone in the interview . . . so I could write a little note . . .
LYDIA	Saying "I hope you've recovered"? Shall I confess something? I had it framed. (*Moves to exit to kitchen, stops.*) You won't go away?
PRINCE	No.
LYDIA	But then . . . you're not really here.
	(*She exits. The* PRINCE *gazes round, then takes out his recorder, switches on and speaks, very softly.*)
PRINCE	"Ten past nine. At Lydia West's."
	(*He is unable to go on. He's spent.* LYDIA *re-enters, hearing him murmuring.*)

LYDIA	What's that?
PRINCE	I've been recording my impressions.
LYDIA	Is that a report on me?
	(*The battles she's had in education come to the fore.*)
PRINCE	Just impressions . . . of the people I've met . . .
LYDIA	Isn't that the same thing?
	(*The kettle whistles. She exits. Someone taps at the door.* JENNY, *neighbour from above, calls out.*)
JENNY	(*off*) Liddy! You in?
	(LYDIA *re-enters. The* PRINCE *stands, Both wonder how to deal with this.*)
	Liddy! Your door's off the latch.
LYDIA	Wait!
	(*But* JENNY *has entered.*)
JENNY	Sorry . . . I'm in! (*Sees* PRINCE.) Oh!
LYDIA	This is a friend of mine.
	(*She wonders how to introduce him.*)
PRINCE	Stuart . . .
	(LYDIA *is caught slightly off guard but recovers.*)
LYDIA	Stuart. This is Jenny from above.
PRINCE	Ahs it goin' Jenny?
	(LYDIA *finds the accent less than convincing.*)
LYDIA	He's from London.
	(JENNY *is sizing him up, taking it as a boyfriend situation.*)

JENNY	Ooh. Thought you might have gone. Only wanted the hairdrier again. Sorry. Oh weren't you outside? Weren't you standing outside in the street, a while ago?

(*The* PRINCE *takes the opportunity to dispel ny notion that he's been there all night.*)

PRINCE	Yeah . . . I'd just got here an I thought it was a bit early fer ringin' the bell.
JENNY	Isn't he considerate? That's very thoughtful. Not like the milkman . . . I'll leave the hairdrier . . .

(LYDIA *gestures and exits for it, very reluctant to leave them alone.*)

You just arrived then?

PRINCE	Jus' arrived *here*, yeah.
JENNY	You must have been cold out there!
PRINCE	I walked a bit . . . You gorra little park.
JENNY	Nice little park . . . which reminds me I never go in it.

(LYDIA *returns with a hairdrier.*)

I've got a job interview.

LYDIA	Good! Where?
JENNY	Portmans. (*To* PRINCE.) Computers. I used to be a nurse. Staff nurse. You get so sick of being thought a sucker. So I got out into selling computers, feeling very guilty . . . but I needn't have 'cos I lost the job. I wouldn't go back to nursing though . . . it's such a battle these days. (*Takes the hairdrier.*) Thanks . . . give it to you tonight.
LYDIA	Not to worry.

(*A pause.*)

JENNY (*about to go*) And what about your soulmate? The Prince! I call him her soulmate. Did you see her lynch him on TV? So what's he done? Sun says he's got a woman in the States. (*To* PRINCE.) She thinks I'm a Royal groupie. I love all these twists and turns of fate in their lives . . . should be sorry for them really. They may have all that they have but they are human. I mean, you don't have your knife in 'em do you Stuart? Not like her . . .

PRINCE Not really.

JENNY Well, they're all having kittens now, poor souls, but I find it exciting. I want to know what's going to happen next. She tears them to pieces! (*Imitates.*) "Not another pissin' skiing holiday!" I don't care, I like them. They put the cherry on top, you know? Bye-bye Stuart.

PRINCE Bye Jenny.

(*She exits.*)

LYDIA She's going to pick up the paper and realise who you are.

(*He doesn't answer this.*)

PRINCE What have you been doing? Since the programme?

LYDIA Trying to live it down. I think they'd have liked me dismissed. Some of the parents did . . . the mothers. There were mothers actually fighting at the school gates . . . pro and anti-Royal. It's strange, I didn't think it was something that would rouse such hate.

PRINCE Nor did I.

(*She knows what he means.*)

LYDIA I don't hate you.

(She exits briefly and returns with the tea. He sips.)

PRINCE   Thank you. *(Sips.)* Ah! The last tea I had was at the bus station and was only fit to be taken intravenously. You said on the programme that there was a lot of poverty among the school parents . . .

LYDIA   The rule of thumb measure is how many get free meals.

PRINCE   Oh?

LYDIA   Yes, well . . . if they qualify for free school dinners then parents are below the poverty line. So out of my class of twenty five there's fourteen get free dinners . . . that's over a third.

PRINCE   I did the first paid work of my life yesterday . . . round about dawn. Polished the floor of a shop . . .

LYDIA   You!

PRINCE   Me. I got the equivalent of a pound for fifteen minutes work . . .

LYDIA   That's very good!

PRINCE   What's the normal rate?

LYDIA   Can be less than two pounds an hour. Some of the Bangladeshi women who work early shifts for contract cleaners told me that's what they got.

PRINCE   Bangladesh. A Commonwealth country . . .

LYDIA   Well, that was always a sham, wasn't it?

PRINCE   I know I've been hopelessly over-protected but this walkabout has affected me much more than I expected. It's not just what people have

	said . . . it's how I've seen them live. To me, of course, to live in a house on a noisy street where vast juggernauts go bouncing within ten feet of the front door . . . that would be the pit of hell . . . I'm saying, for me . . .
LYDIA	Probably is for them!
PRINCE	My great uncle Edward tried to do something about poverty in the last depression. He went round the South Wales coal fields . . . talked to the unemployed . . . saw the slums and spoke out about it. I know he went off the rails later and started flirting with Nazi-ism . . . but what I'm saying is he was political. Should I be?
LYDIA	Depends which direction.
PRINCE	Come out strongly. Say it is unacceptable that a country so rich should still tolerate poverty.
LYDIA	They'll say we're not rich.
PRINCE	You mean the rich will say we're not rich? Well . . . tell me. Should the monarchy do it? Become political? Take the thing by the scruff of the neck and shake it . . .
LYDIA	No.
PRINCE	Why not?
LYDIA	Because *we* should do it.
PRINCE	But I can't spend my life doing nothing about the things that matter! Be some blessed mime or mute in a glittering show and say damn all about what goes on beyond the scenery! The finger points at me, I've won the lottery . . . what do I do with the prize?
LYDIA	Tell them you don't want it!

(*He stares at her, wrestling with the problem. Then he stands.*)

PRINCE	I must leave.
LYDIA	No! You mustn't go so soon! Have I offended you?
PRINCE	Not in any way. You've helped me.
LYDIA	Then stay. You're exhausted. Sleep here. I'll go to work. No one will disturb you. There's no one else here. Don't you remember the tabloids? I'm a 'single mother'. (*She wonders if he knew that.*) I'll be back at four with my daughter. Please! Then Cathy will have seen a prince.
PRINCE	You know what they'd make of it . . . the press.
LYDIA	I know how to deal with them after last time.
PRINCE	But you weren't in the position of having fifty thousand pounds waved under your nose . . . and being pressured to tell them the story they wanted to hear. You send them packing . . . they move on to Jenny. She won't talk . . . they find your ex-partner. He keeps faith . . . they ambush Cathy's playgroup leader. They write the story . . . it's only a matter of getting it initialled. Look . . . I've already made arrangements. This is the end of my journey.
LYDIA	I was so grim at that interview. I haven't said the things I should have said.
PRINCE	Then we'll write to each other. There's no reason in the world why we shouldn't see each other. If Cathy and you were invited to . . . an event . . . would you come?
LYDIA	What? A garden party?
PRINCE	Something less starchy. Would you?
LYDIA	Yes.
PRINCE	All we are is the cherry on top.

ACT TWO

> (*He embraces her, and as they draw apart, a fade to black.*)

Scene Nine

Nearly sunset. Twilight birdsong. A field. Deep countryside, probably near Sandringham. We discover SKIP *and* RON MCNEIL. *They've arrived in a Range Rover to meet with the* PRINCE. MCNEIL *stares through field glasses.*

RON Nothing on the road. His highness couldn't have named the wrong field, could he sir?

SKIP This is the place. He knows this spot.

RON You see, sir, to me it looks the same as the field next door.

 (*He gestures.*)

SKIP We both know it by the view. From the trees on the hill to the steeple. This was our getting over the wall spot. Well, not so far over the wall.

RON If he doesn't come soon, sir, we'll have to put out a search.

SKIP We stay put. That was my promise. We stay here if we have to stay till the moon comes up. He specifically asked you to drive me here, sergeant, on the basis that you wouldn't speak to anyone or raise the alarm. He doesn't want a reception committee.

RON What worries me, sir, is that he could easily take another road . . .

SKIP No. Train to King's Lynn, mini-cab to the village . . . then he'll walk. And that's the road.

RON Something over there.

(They look off to the side.)

Someone climbing the fence . . .

SKIP   *(recognising who it is)* Certainly is . . .

RON   *(realises)* So that's what he was wearing.

SKIP   *(calls)* Hey!

PRINCE   *(off)* Hey!

(The PRINCE enters, in high spirits.)

All done . . . and in one piece . . . sergeant! I hope you didn't get a roasting . . .

RON   No sir. The Inspector understood.

SKIP   You look like someone out of a booze commercial.

(The brothers whoop and embrace.)

PRINCE   You get high on actually doing something of your own absolutely free will! I'm sorry sergeant . . . it is good to see you.

RON   Ditto sir. I'll be by the car . . .

PRINCE   No radioing for the moment . . .

RON   No sir.

(He exits to Land Rover.)

SKIP   I didn't want to trust McNeil.

PRINCE   No, no. I wanted him here. We can do all the necessary before we have to face everyone.

SKIP   You really alright?

PRINCE   Never better! I had an almighty sleep on the train. Incredible dreams!

SKIP   I thought you'd be mugged.

PRINCE   I was!

SKIP   Christ!

PRINCE   Well . . . a small mug. Bit of a bruise here.

(*He rubs his stomach.*)

Knee in the Royal groin.

SKIP   Who did it?

PRINCE   Our side. Well he said he was on our side.

SKIP   He knew you?

PRINCE   (*east London*) Knew me? No chance mate . . . leave it aht!

SKIP   I thought you'd go doolally . . .

PRINCE   There's no point in pretending I've come back from this as I went out.

(SKIP *wants to know the decision.*)

SKIP   So . . .

PRINCE   I'm not taking it on, Skip.

(SKIP *expects this but it still hits him emotionally.*)

SKIP   Thought so. That famous letter of yours . . . it practically said it anyway. You could have saved yourself a trip.

PRINCE   No, no. The trip was part of the decision. I walked to wear out the excuses. Miles of pavements! I did it to lay the pretence that it wasn't up to me. I've seen such places. Small town at night, where for a while I seemed the only soul awake! Bedroom windows not much higher from me than my upstretched hand. I could hear them sigh in their sleep, I was so close! There was a man crying by his front door . . . half cut . . . two in the morning. I think his wife had locked him out. He saw me.

	Two of us in that street. He said "Fuck off" but it wasn't what he meant. His eyes! What possible sense does it make for him to be my "subject"?
SKIP	Might to him . . .
PRINCE	It's his world! He's got to possess it!
SKIP	I don't know what that means.
PRINCE	(*lets this pass*) What have they been saying?
SKIP	You know what old whatsisname used to say, "Bloody minefield without a map". Bit like that.
PRINCE	And . . . ?
SKIP	Well, there was a wall-to-wall family conference. Wow! Your letter read and read. Me questioned. What amazed me was how they'd all pretty well thought alike. Oh there was some grief and woe. A few crusty tantrums . . .
PRINCE	Ah yes.
SKIP	But not grandmother. She'd seen it coming. Anyway, it was decided that after her Golden Jubilee, two years from now . . . 2002 . . . the family's ready to hand over to whoever they put up . . .
PRINCE	But we announce it now?
SKIP	Yes . . . I think . . . yes, right away. You'll have your chance to talk about it first . . . then it's Prime Minister time. Oh . . . someone who shall be nameless said, "I'd have sooner we surrendered to the Conservatives!"
PRINCE	And no one's going to break ranks? Don't want them digging out someone who's forty third in line who says, "I'll do it! I'll do it!"

SKIP They say Parliament could do that. They could give it to Lord Sutch if they wanted to.

PRINCE Or send for foreign royalty . . . we were foreign royalty once.

SKIP No . . . it got talked about. All the usual cousin jokes. But no.

PRINCE You see . . . I saw two choices. One was to do what no politician would want me to do, to bring the monarchy back into politics. To make it clear that one was going to make a fuss about the things one saw as wrong in the realm. I met an old lady, late at night who dared me to kill her . . .

SKIP Why?

PRINCE Because she wanted some release, I suppose. You come away with a score of voices in your head . . . all with stories of such pain and individual suffering . . . and you feel helpless. The situation makes you helpless! Do I go through that and come back and live just as I did before?

SKIP They'd never let you be political . . .

PRINCE Not the politicians, no. And in a way it would be dangerously easy. The politicians' credit out there is on the floor. There are too many who'd like someone to rise above them . . . "incorruptible"! We know what lies down that route . . . no. I think the other choice is the only one.

SKIP But they still want us . . .

PRINCE But should they want us? The country has to know itself. To know its own face. And I mean the English, especially. Far clearer for the Scots, the Welsh and Irish to know themselves than the English. All that massive muddled history in the way. An uncertain people caught

between two powers . . . America sucking
away our culture . . . Europe sucking away the
rest. That's why they cling to us . . . as a kind
of pseudo-identity. A substitute religion. An
escape . . . I could hear it in everyone I spoke
to . . . a dressing up box to hide the nation's
nakedness. But we are what we see in the
glass! And that's what we must be.

(*The sun is setting.*)

You can't think how I look forward to
tomorrow. Look at this country! Why does
everyone have to talk about it as though it's
weighed down with its past? It's young . . .
not old. It's we who have made it seem old.

(MCNEIL *enters from the direction of the road.*)

MCNEIL Excuse me sir . . . I can't hold off much
longer . . . I'm overdue reporting in.

(MCNEIL *has his portable. The* PRINCE *indicates it.*)

PRINCE Yes . . . so am I.

(MCNEIL *dials him the number and listens. Then he gets through.*)

MCNEIL (*into phone*) His Royal Highness . . . one
moment.

(*As he hands the phone to the* PRINCE, *a fade to black.*)

Scene Ten

The lobby of the House of Commons. Various members in a hurry. JAMES *sees* JO *passing and crosses to her.*

JAMES Jo! We've got twenty thousand people in
Trafalgar Square, which is not bad for a week

	day. I had quite a job getting to the House. I heard you gave a fine speech this afternoon. Well done!
Jo	It's not well done. I see nothing well done. The whole thing's a walking disaster!
James	Look, I know you're not getting all you wanted but think how far we've come! It's only six months since we started the campaign. Two weeks later the royal family bow out. Now, here we are with the second reading of a Republican Bill!
Jo	It is not a Republican Bill as I've been saying in there for the past three days! You read through that bill and you won't find the word 'Republic' in it anywhere . . . a Labour front bench and a Labour Prime Minister afraid to use the word 'Republic'. Some of them actually want to get round it the Australian way by calling Britain a Commonwealth . . . despite the fact that we've got no wealth and it certainly isn't held in common!
James	But everyone outside Parliament is calling it a Republic . . . go and ask them in Trafalgar Square, ask them in Cardiff and Glasgow.
Jo	But the lack of popular election, James! That's the issue. The whole idea behind the move away from monarchy was to strengthen democracy! Yet what do we have? The government . . . my party's government . . . says no. Direct election would give the president too much power over the Prime Minister . . . so the government want to nominate the candidate, and Parliament will vote . . . and only Parliament! The Head of State will be the Prime Minister's poodle!

(CARL POINTER, *crossing the lobby, has joined them.*)

DIVINE RIGHT

CARL: Well . . . that's the deal, isn't it? It's a stitch up between your front bench and ours. Both party leaders want exactly the same thing . . . a Head of State with as much authority as a car park attendant . . .

JO: We shouldn't have trusted the cabinet. Just when you think you've built up enough support there, they go away in secret and it all evaporates!

JAMES: Obviously the government wants the House united . . . and, whenever Parliament unites, you know it's up to no good . . .

CARL: God help us . . . they're even trying to hang on to the royals . . . they'll still have Buck House and Windsor and be trotted out on State occasions if the Cabinet has its way . . . and the old country house culture will go rolling on . . . we could have headed for clear water and we've just found another part of the swamp! What happened to the party of revolution, Jo?

JO: It made itself fit to govern, didn't it?

CARL: The only clear cut radical notion of the past thirty years has come from our side of the House. What a time to be out of power!

(JAMES *sees the* PRIME MINISTER *crossing the lobby*.)

JAMES: (*to* JO) Isn't that your leader?

JO: Ah! Excuse me . . .

(*She moves to the* PM *and buttonholes him*.)

Prime Minister!

PM: There's only one thing I'd like to hear from you, Jo, and that's that you and your supporters are voting for the bill . . .

Jo	The group's meeting in five minutes to decide.
PM	And I hope it decides that this is no time for gesture politics . . .
Jo	We were never properly consulted! You call yourself a moderniser . . . that means sweeping the old trappings away not harbouring them!
PM	I'm in a hurry now. Yes, I'm a moderniser . . . and that means modernising . . . not destroying. You don't modernise a Victorian building by bulldozing it down. Do you think a republic will be popular . . . when so many people — ordinary people — have given their lives for king, queen and country? This measure was forced on us and frankly it's a bloody nuisance. Thousands of hours of legislative time will be wasted because of it and millions of pounds. Time and money that could be spent on health, education and jobs. There was a radical agenda, Jo, but you were too blinkered to see it . . . and now you and the fall of the House of Windsor have set it back years. So don't make life harder for me than it already is. Get real and get me those votes.

(*He continues on his way.* JAMES *and* CARL *join her.*)

Jo	He's not going to smile me that smile and tell me he wants our votes. He's not going to get them!
JAMES	Jo!
Jo	I'm going to try to persuade the group to vote against . . .
JAMES	But it'll send the wrong signals, the country sees it as the Republican Bill . . . for republicans to vote against is not going to be understood. Carl . . .

CARL	Oh I shall vote for. That way I might be better able to get support for a few amendments . . . I shall resort to the traditional weapon of the small minority . . . sheer deviousness!
JO	(*to* JAMES) You're thinking of the campaign. I'm thinking of Parliament. I didn't work to gain a republic just to get rid the monarchy. It's the positive virtues of a presidency that I have to hold out for. And the reason I have to is that the people are so deeply tired of this place and have come to despise all of us . . . the whole profession of politics . . . not because we don't deliver what we promise, but because they suspect that we couldn't if we tried. They think we've lost control over events . . . and over ourselves. A republic can't put those things right . . . but it could announce our intentions. And what a way to announce them if we deny what we know the people want . . . the right to vote for a citizen president who'll have the power to make an honest institution out of Parliament!
JAMES	For my part I've lived long enough to see what I wanted to see . . . the UK become the United Republics of the British Isles . . . that's what it is in effect . . . and before this bill is through that's what they'll have to call it. (*The* PRINCE *has entered the lobby,* MCNEIL *a little way behind.* JAMES *sees him.*) Your highness!
PRINCE	Sir James! (*They shake hands.*)
JAMES	Actually, it's no longer Sir James, your highness.
PRINCE	Well, as far as I'm concerned, it's no longer "your highness".

                (JAMES *is about to introduce the others but the* PRINCE *recognises them. They shake hands.*)

                Jo Benyon . . . Carl Pointer . . . I've seen you so often in the news. The triumphant trio!

CARL   We haven't seen the Bill through yet . . .

PRINCE   But that's a foregone conclusion, isn't it?

JO   (*with feeling*) Yes.

PRINCE   What are they calling it? The Constitutional Reform Bill? Sounds a part of history before it's even through.

JO   Indeed . . .

PRINCE   I doubt if a member of the royal family has ever walked into this lobby before. I'm exercising my right as a citizen to lobby my MP.

CARL   May we ask who that is?

PRINCE   Well it's still unresolved . . . a matter of which residence I'm domiciled in. The others, technically, become 'holiday homes'. Of course, what I'm really here for is to be present at the actual event. See how you go about it. You see, now that I'm a simple citizen, I've been thinking I might pursue a political career in a few years time.

JAMES   In what way?

PRINCE   I thought I might refuse all dukedoms . . . renounce my titles . . . as at least one notable left-winger has done . . . and stand for Parliament.

CARL   I take it you've decided which party?

PRINCE   Oh . . . as an independent, wouldn't you think?

Jo	If you're being serious . . . and I'm not sure you are . . . we ought to put a stop to that.
Prince	Why?
Jo	Because you'd walk it! They'd vote for you in droves!
Carl	And after some years gaining valuable parliamentary experience . . . (*He passes the ball to* James.)
James	You'll end up the perfect candidate for president!
Jo	Which would be most unfair . . .
Prince	Well there you are . . . I'm so ignorant about it. I didn't realise politics were supposed to be fair . . .

(*A slow fade to black.*)

Scene Eleven

House of Commons debating chamber. MPs are finishing voting on the Bill . . . members returning from the lobbies to hear the result declared . . . a relaxed and festive feeling . . . the vote being a foregone conclusion, but the occasion historic.

The tellers approach the Speaker's *chair. They bow and place the result into the* Speaker's *hands. Over this we hear the voice of a TV political commentator.*

Voice	At "the end of the day" as they say it's all down to Westminster . . . and we go back there to see how the house has voted on what some are calling "Britain's second revolution". Let me remind you of the wording of the Bill: it is a bill to transfer the constitutional powers of the monarch to what is called, in a very British way, "a

Parliamentary Head of State". Let no one whisper the word "President".

(*The commentary has faded. The* SPEAKER *reads out from the card.*)

SPEAKER   The ayes to the left . . . four hundred and six. The noes to the right, seventy three. The ayes have it.

(*Through this and the cheers at the result . . . and the general dispersal of members afterwards, we hear the school hall piano at* LYDIA'S *school strike up and the voices of two hundred junior school children singing "Jerusalem", the innocence of their voices contrasting with the knowingness and worldliness of the departing MPs.* JO BENYON *lingers behind, looking around her at the emptying chamber. The lights fade.*)